How do I get a *half price* lesson?

It's easy. Just fill out the form below and we'll give you a half price lesson.

Plus, we're the only national driving school exclusively using fully qualified instructors. And you'll be learning in a Ford Focus with air conditioning and power steering. Best of all, when you pre-pay for a course of 12 hours, we'll give you a £24 discount, 1 year's free AA breakdown cover worth around £47 (Option 100)* and a £100 holiday voucher.* Great value. A great instructor. And a great car. You get it all.

*Terms and conditions apply.

Just **AA** sk.

AA driving school
0800 60 70 80
www.theAA.com

Half price lesson voucher

Complete this voucher and hand it to your instructor at the start of your first lesson.

Name _____

Pupil Number (given on calling 0800 60 70 80)_____

I apply for my half price hour of driving tuition and confirm I am not an existing pupil of AA driving school.

Signed _____

For Instructor Use Only:

Instructor Name_____ Instructor Number_____

AA Driving Test

THEORY

The **Official**
Questions
& Answers

AA Publishing

Produced by AA Publishing.
© Automobile Developments Limited 2001
First edition 1996
Reprinted 1996 (5 times)
Second edition with revised questions 1997
Reprinted 1998 (twice)
Third edition with revised questions 1998
Reprinted with amendments 1998 (twice)
Fourth edition with revised questions 1999
Reprinted 2000
Fifth edition with revised questions 2000
Sixth edition with revised questions 2001
Reprinted 2002 (twice) and June 2002 with amendment

ISBN 0 7495 3445 1

Published by AA Publishing (a trading name of Automobile
Association Developments Limited, whose registered office is
Millstream, Maidenhead Road, Windsor, SL4 5GD; registered
number 1878835).

The AA's Web site address is ***www.theAA.com***

The contents of this book are believed correct at the time of
printing. Nevertheless, the publishers cannot be held
responsible for any errors or omissions or for changes in the
details given in this book or for the consequences of any
reliance on the information provided by the same.

Colour separation by Anton Graphics, Andover.
Printed in Italy by G. Canale & C. s.p.a., Turin.
Editor: Jane Gregory.

> While every effort has been made to include
> the widest possible range of questions
> available at the time of printing, the
> Government may from time to time change,
> add or remove questions, and the publisher
> cannot be held responsible for questions that
> may appear on a question paper which were
> not available for inclusion in this book.

Contents

THE THEORY TEST & HPT

About the Theory Test

You now have to pass two driving tests before you can apply for a full driving licence. The Theory Test was introduced in 1996, and this book contains the official questions from the DSA (Driving Standards Agency) that you may have to answer. You will have to pass both the question part and the video part (or HPT – see below) to pass your Theory Test, before you can apply for the Practical Test.

Your questions answered

Q. *Why a Theory Test?*
A. To check that drivers know more than just how to operate a car.
Q. *How does it work?*
A. The test consists of 35 multiple-choice questions, and a separate video clips section (see below for more about HPT).
Q. *What is a multiple-choice question?*
A. One with 4, 5 or 6 answers to choose from.
Q. *What do the questions cover?*
A. All the topics listed in this book.

The Theory Test questions

You will have 40 minutes to complete the question part of the test, using a touch-screen, and all questions are multiple-choice. The Government may change the pass mark from time to time. Your driving school will be able to tell you if there has been a change. Also, the Government may, from time to time, introduce new or amended questions. However, if you are fully prepared on each topic, you will be in a position to answer any question.

About this book

This book will help you to pass the questions section of your Theory Test:

- the introduction provides useful advice and information.
- the questions and answers are arranged under the 14 official syllabus topics.
- questions dealing with related aspects of a topic are grouped together.
- all the correct answers are at the back of the book.

How to use this book

1. Look at the list of topics on page 5 and turn t one you find interesting.
2. Read the first question and tick your choice o answer(s).
3. Check your answer(s) against the correct answers at the back of the book.
4. Make sure you understand the answer(s) before you try the next question.

Warning

Do **not** try too many questions at once.
Do **not** try to learn the answers by heart.
The order of the answers in this book may be different from how they are arranged in the actual test – so do **not** try to memorise the order.

How to answer the questions

Each questions has four, five or six answers. You must mark the boxes with the correct answer or answers. Each question tells you how many answer to mark.

Study each question carefully, making sure you understand. Look carefully at any diagram, drawing or photograph. Before you look at the answers given, decide what you think the right answer may be. You can then select the answer that matches th one you had decided on. If you follow this system, you will avoid being confused by answers that appear to be similar.

The Hazard Perception Test

Towards the end of 2002, the Theory Test will be extended to include HPT. HPT stands for Hazard Perception Test, and you will need to pass both the questions and the video test to get a pass in your Theory Test.

More about HPT

The aim of the Hazard Perception Test is to find ou how quickly you are able to detect developing hazards coming up on the road ahead. A hazard is anything that might cause you to change speed or direction when driving. HPT has been added to make sure that new drivers know all about hazards and how to look out for them before they are allowed to drive on their own. Learner drivers need more training in how to spot hazards, because they are often so busy thinking about using the car's controls that they forget to watch the road and traffic. Proper training can really help you to see more of the hazards that you will meet when driving, and to see those hazards earlier. If you have good hazard perception skills you are much less likely to have an accident.

What happens in the HPT test?

First you will get a short talk explaining how the test works; you will also get a chance to practice with the computer and mouse before you start the test 'for real'. This is to make sure that you know what to expect, and that you are happy with what you need to do.

Then you will see video clips of a real street scene with traffic such as motor vehicles, pedestrians and cyclists. The scenes are shot from the point of view of a driver in a car. You have to notice hazards that are developing on the road ahead – that is, problems that could lead to an accident. As soon as you see a hazard coming up in the video clip, you click the mouse control. You score points depending on how quickly you are able to identify the developing hazard.

Your questions about HPT answered

Q. *How long is the HPT test?*

A. The test lasts about 20 minutes.

Q. *How many hazards should I be able to spot?*

A. You should find 15 hazards to 'click' on during the 20 minutes.

Q. *Can I see the real video clips before I take the test, so that I can practice?*

A. You won't be able to practice with the real video clips used in the test. This is because HPT tests how fast you can spot and react to hazards. If you had seen the actual clips before, it would not be a realistic or useful test.

Q. *So how can I prepare for the HPT?*

A. Your driver instructor has been trained to help you learn hazard perception skills, and can give you plenty of practice in

● what to look out for when driving.

● how to anticipate hazards.

● what action to take when you have to deal with hazards of all kinds.

A practice video and workbook will be made available – check with your driving instructor.

Preparing for both tests

You are strongly recommended to prepare for the Theory Test at the same time as you develop your skills behind the wheel for the Practical Test. Obviously, there are many similarities between the two tests – it is all about helping to make you a safer driver on today's busy roads. By preparing for both tests at the same time, you will reinforce your knowledge and understanding of all aspects of driving and you will improve your chances of passing both tests first time.

Selecting a driving school

When you select a driving school to teach you the practical skills, make sure they are prepared to advise and help you with the Theory Test. Good driving schools will provide theory practice papers for you to complete before you take the real test. These papers will help you judge your level of knowledge and help with your preparation. Check with friends who have been taught recently, and make sure you understand the difference between an instructor who displays a pink badge or licence (a trainee instructor) and one who displays a green badge or licence (a fully qualified instructor). Price is important, so find out whether the school offers any discounts for blocks or courses of lessons paid in advance; if you decide to pay in advance, make sure the driving school is reputable. If lesson prices are very low, ask yourself 'why?' Check how long the lesson will last, some driving schools offer lessons of less than 60 minutes. And don't forget to ask about the car you'll be learning to drive in. Is it modern and reliable? Is it insured? Has it dual controls?

What to expect

As with all courses, there are a number of subjects you will need to master. All good driving schools will have available a progress sheet and syllabus which sets out all the skills you will need and keeps a record of your progress. You will probably find that if you take a two-hour lesson every week, your rate of progress will surprise you!

It is important that you should not take your Theory Test too early in your course of practical lessons. This is because you need the experience of meeting real hazards while you are learning to drive, so that you will be able to pass the HPT part of the Theory Test. However, you must pass the Theory Test before you can take the Practical Test. Agree a plan of action with your driving instructor.

After a few hours of driving tuition the instructor will discuss with you a structured course to suit your needs and you can agree on the likely date when you will be ready to take the Practical Test. Once you have passed your Theory Test, you can apply for a Practical Test appointment; this will give you added incentive to prepare thoroughly.

The AA Driving School

The AA has a driving school that only uses fully qualified instructors, who are all familiar with this book, the Theory Test and the Practical Test. Why not give them a try? You can ring for details on freephone **0800 60 70 80** or visit the website at **www.theAA.com**.

Knowledge, skills and attitude

Being a good driver is more than just having the knowledge and the skills – it is about applying them with the right attitude. No one is a 'natural' or a 'perfect driver'. All drivers make mistakes. Being careful, courteous and considerate to other road users will complement the skills and knowledge you will acquire in the coming weeks and make you a good driver.

1 Before you make a U-turn in the road, you should

Mark one answer

- [ ] A. give an arm signal as well as using your indicators
- [ ] B. signal so that other drivers can slow down for you
- [x] C. look over your shoulder for a final check
- [ ] D. select a higher gear than normal

2 As you approach this bridge you should

Mark three answers

- [ ] A. move into the middle of the road to get a better view
- [x] B. slow down
- [ ] C. get over the bridge as quickly as possible
- [x] D. consider using your horn
- [ ] E. find another route
- [x] F. beware of pedestrians

3 When following a large vehicle you should keep well back because

Mark one answer

- [ ] A. it allows you to corner more quickly
- [ ] B. it helps the large vehicle to stop more easily
- [x] C. it allows the driver to see you in the mirrors
- [ ] D. it helps you to keep out of the wind

4 In which of these situations should you avoid overtaking?

Mark one answer

- [ ] A. Just after a bend
- [ ] B. In a one-way street
- [ ] C. On a 30mph road
- [x] D. Approaching a dip in the road

5 This road marking warns

Mark one answer

- [ ] A. drivers to use the hard shoulder
- [ ] B. overtaking drivers there is a bend to the left
- [x] C. overtaking drivers to move back to the left
- [ ] D. drivers that it is safe to overtake

6 Your mobile phone rings while you are travelling. You should

Mark one answer
- A. stop immediately
- B. answer it immediately
- [✓] C. pull up in a suitable place
- D. pull up at the nearest kerb

7 Why are these yellow lines painted across the road?

Mark one answer
- A. To help you choose the correct lane
- B. To help you keep the correct separation distance
- [✓] C. To make you aware of your speed
- D. To tell you the distance to the roundabout

8 You are approaching traffic lights that have been on green for some time. You should

Mark one answer
- A. accelerate hard
- B. maintain your speed
- [✓] C. be ready to stop
- D. brake hard

9 Which of the following should you do before stopping?

Mark one answer
- A. Sound the horn
- [✓] B. Use the mirrors
- C. Select a higher gear
- D. Flash your headlights

10 As a driver what does the term 'Blind Spot' mean?

Mark one answer
- A. An area covered by your right hand mirror
- B. An area not covered by your headlights
- C. An area covered by your left hand mirror
- [✓] D. An area not seen in your mirrors

11 Objects hanging from your interior mirror may

Mark two answers
- [✓] A. restrict your view
- B. improve your driving
- [✓] C. distract your attention
- D. help your concentration

12 Which of the following may cause loss of concentration on a long journey?

Mark four answers
- [✓] A. Loud music
- [✓] B. Arguing with a passenger
- [✓] C. Using a mobile phone
- [✓] D. Putting in a cassette tape
- E. Stopping regularly to rest
- F. Pulling up to tune the radio

13 On a long motorway journey boredom can cause you to feel sleepy. You should

Mark two answers

- ☑ **A.** leave the motorway and find a safe place to stop
- ☐ **B.** keep looking around at the surrounding landscape
- ☐ **C.** drive faster to complete your journey sooner
- ☑ **D.** ensure a supply of fresh air into your vehicle
- ☐ **E.** stop on the hard shoulder for a rest

14 You are driving at dusk. You should switch your lights on

Mark two answers

- ☑ **A.** even when street lights are not lit
- ☑ **B.** so others can see you
- ☐ **C.** only when others have done so
- ☐ **D.** only when street lights are lit

15 You are most likely to lose concentration when driving if you

Mark two answers

- ☑ **A.** use a mobile phone
- ☑ **B.** listen to very loud music
- ☐ **C.** switch on the heated rear window
- ☐ **D.** look at the door mirrors

16 Which FOUR are most likely to cause you to lose concentration while you are driving?

Mark four answers

- ☑ **A.** Using a mobile phone
- ☑ **B.** Talking into a microphone
- ☑ **C.** Tuning your car radio
- ☑ **D.** Looking at a map
- ☐ **E.** Checking the mirrors
- ☐ **F.** Using the demisters

17 You should not use a mobile phone whilst driving

Mark one answer

- ☐ **A.** until you are satisfied that no other traffic is near
- ☐ **B.** unless you are able to drive one-handed
- ☑ **C.** because it might distract your attention from the road ahead
- ☐ **D.** because reception is poor when the engine is running

18 Your vehicle is fitted with a hands-free phone system. Using this equipment whilst driving

Mark one answer

- ☐ **A.** is quite safe as long as you slow down
- ☑ **B.** could distract your attention from the road
- ☐ **C.** is recommended by *The Highway Code*
- ☐ **D.** could be very good for road safety

19 Using a hands-free phone is likely to

Mark one answer

- [ ] **A.** improve your safety
- [ ] **B.** increase your concentration
- [ ] **C.** reduce your view
- [✓] **D.** divert your attention

20 You should ONLY use a mobile phone when

Mark one answer

- [ ] **A.** receiving a call
- [✓] **B.** suitably parked
- [ ] **C.** driving at less than 30mph
- [ ] **D.** driving an automatic vehicle

21 Using a mobile phone while you are driving

Mark one answer

- [ ] **A.** is acceptable in a vehicle with power steering
- [ ] **B.** will reduce your field of vision
- [✓] **C.** could distract your attention from the road
- [ ] **D.** will affect your vehicle's electronic systems

22 What is the safest way to use a mobile phone in your vehicle?

Mark one answer

- [ ] **A.** Use hands-free equipment
- [✓] **B.** Find a suitable place to stop
- [ ] **C.** Drive slowly on a quiet road
- [ ] **D.** Direct your call through the operator

23 You are driving on a wet road. You have to stop your vehicle in an emergency. You should

Mark one answer

- [ ] **A.** apply the handbrake and footbrake together
- [✓] **B.** keep both hands on the wheel
- [ ] **C.** select reverse gear
- [ ] **D.** give an arm signal

24 When you are moving off from behind a parked car you should

Mark three answers

- [✓] **A.** look round before you move off
- [✓] **B.** use all the mirrors on the vehicle
- [ ] **C.** look round after moving off
- [ ] **D.** use the exterior mirrors only
- [✓] **E.** give a signal if necessary
- [ ] **F.** give a signal after moving off

25 You are travelling along this narrow country road. When passing the cyclist you should go

Mark one answer

- [ ] **A.** slowly, sounding the horn as you pass
- [ ] **B.** quickly, leaving plenty of room
- [✓] **C.** slowly, leaving plenty of room
- [ ] **D.** quickly, sounding the horn as you pass

26 Your vehicle is fitted with a hand-held telephone. To use the telephone you should

Mark one answer

- A. reduce your speed
- ☑ B. find a safe place to stop
- C. steer the vehicle with one hand
- D. be particularly careful at junctions

27 To answer a call on your mobile phone while travelling you should

Mark one answer

- A. reduce your speed wherever you are
- ☑ B. stop in a proper and convenient place
- C. keep the call time to a minimum
- D. slow down and allow others to overtake

28 Your mobile phone rings while you are on the motorway. Before answering you should

Mark one answer

- A. reduce your speed to 50mph
- B. pull up on the hard shoulder
- C. move into the left-hand lane
- ☑ D. stop in a safe place

29 A pelican crossing that crosses the road in a STRAIGHT line and has a central island MUST be treated as

Mark one answer
- [ ] A. one crossing in daylight only
- [✓] B. one complete crossing
- [ ] C. two separate crossings
- [ ] D. two crossings during darkness

30 At a pelican crossing the flashing amber light means you MUST

Mark one answer
- [ ] A. stop and wait for the green light
- [ ] B. stop and wait for the red light
- [ ] C. give way to pedestrians waiting to cross
- [✓] D. give way to pedestrians already on the crossing

31 You are approaching a pelican crossing. The amber light is flashing. You MUST

Mark one answer
- [✓] A. give way to pedestrians who are crossing
- [ ] B. encourage pedestrians to cross
- [ ] C. not move until the green light appears
- [ ] D. stop even if the crossing is clear

32 You should never wave people across at pedestrian crossings because

Mark one answer
- [✓] A. there may be another vehicle coming
- [ ] B. they may not be looking
- [ ] C. it is safer for you to carry on
- [ ] D. they may not be ready to cross

33 At a puffin crossing what colour follows the green signal?

Mark one answer
- [ ] A. Steady red
- [ ] B. Flashing amber
- [✓] C. Steady amber
- [ ] D. Flashing green

34 You could use the 'Two-Second Rule'

Mark one answer
- [ ] A. before restarting the engine after it has stalled
- [✓] B. to keep a safe gap from the vehicle in front
- [ ] C. before using the 'Mirror-Signal-Manoeuvre' routine
- [ ] D. when emerging on wet roads

35 'Tailgating' means

Mark one answer
- [ ] A. using the rear door of a hatchback car
- [ ] B. reversing into a parking space
- [✓] C. following another vehicle too closely
- [ ] D. driving with rear fog lights on

36 Following this vehicle too closely is unwise because

Mark one answer
- [ ] A. your brakes will overheat
- [ ] B. your view ahead is increased
- [ ] C. your engine will overheat
- [✓] D. your view ahead is reduced

37 You are following a vehicle on a wet road. You should leave a time gap of at least

Mark one answer

- [ ] A. one second
- [ ] B. two seconds
- [ ] C. three seconds
- [✓] D. four seconds

38 You are in a line of traffic. The driver behind you is following very closely. What action should you take?

Mark one answer

- [ ] A. Ignore the following driver and continue to drive within the speed limit
- [✓] B. Slow down, gradually increasing the gap between you and the vehicle in front
- [ ] C. Signal left and wave the following driver past
- [ ] D. Move over to a position just left of the centre line of the road

39 A long, heavily-laden lorry is taking a long time to overtake you. What should you do?

Mark one answer

- [ ] A. Speed up
- [✓] B. Slow down
- [ ] C. Hold your speed
- [ ] D. Change direction

40 Which of the following vehicles will use blue flashing beacons?

Mark three answers

- [ ] A. Motorway maintenance
- [✓] B. Bomb disposal
- [✓] C. Blood transfusion
- [✓] D. Police patrol
- [ ] E. Breakdown recovery

41 Which THREE of these emergency services might have blue flashing beacons?

Mark three answers

- [✓] A. Coastguard
- [✓] B. Bomb disposal
- [ ] C. Gritting lorries
- [ ] D. Animal ambulances
- [✓] E. Mountain rescue
- [ ] F. Doctors' cars

42 When being followed by an ambulance showing a flashing blue beacon you should

Mark one answer

- [✓] A. pull over as soon as safely possible to let it pass
- [ ] B. accelerate hard to get away from it
- [ ] C. maintain your speed and course
- [ ] D. brake harshly and immediately stop in the road

43 What type of emergency vehicle is fitted with a green flashing beacon?

Mark one answer
- [ ] **A.** Fire engine
- [ ] **B.** Road gritter
- [ ] **C.** Ambulance
- [x] **D.** Doctor's car

44 A flashing green beacon on a vehicle means

Mark one answer
- [ ] **A.** police on non-urgent duties
- [x] **B.** doctor on an emergency call
- [ ] **C.** road safety patrol operating
- [ ] **D.** gritting in progress

45 A vehicle has a flashing green beacon. What does this mean?

Mark one answer
- [x] **A.** A doctor is answering an emergency call
- [ ] **B.** The vehicle is slow-moving
- [ ] **C.** It is a motorway police patrol vehicle
- [ ] **D.** A vehicle is carrying hazardous chemicals

46 Diamond-shaped signs give instructions to

Mark one answer
- [x] **A.** tram drivers
- [ ] **B.** bus drivers
- [ ] **C.** lorry drivers
- [ ] **D.** taxi drivers

47 On a road where trams operate, which of these vehicles will be most at risk from the tram rails?

Mark one answer
- [ ] **A.** Cars
- [x] **B.** Cycles
- [ ] **C.** Buses
- [ ] **D.** Lorries

48 What should you use your horn for?

Mark one answer
- [x] **A.** To alert others to your presence
- [ ] **B.** To allow you right of way
- [ ] **C.** To greet other road users
- [ ] **D.** To signal your annoyance

49 You are in a one-way street and want to turn right. You should position yourself

Mark one answer
- [x] **A.** in the right-hand lane
- [ ] **B.** in the left-hand lane
- [ ] **C.** in either lane, depending on the traffic
- [ ] **D.** just left of the centre line

50 You wish to turn right ahead. Why should you take up the correct position in good time?

Mark one answer
- [ ] **A.** To allow other drivers to pull out in front of you
- [ ] **B.** To give a better view into the road that you're joining
- [x] **C.** To help other road users know what you intend to do
- [ ] **D.** To allow drivers to pass you on the right

51 At which type of crossing are cyclists allowed to ride across with pedestrians?

Mark one answer

- ☑ **A.** Toucan
- ☐ **B.** Puffin
- ☐ **C.** Pelican
- ☐ **D.** Zebra

52 A bus is stopped at a bus stop ahead of you. Its right-hand indicator is flashing. You should

Mark one answer

- ☐ **A.** flash your headlights and slow down
- ☑ **B.** slow down and give way if it is safe to do so
- ☐ **C.** sound your horn and keep going
- ☐ **D.** slow down and then sound your horn

53 You are travelling at the legal speed limit. A vehicle comes up quickly behind, flashing its headlights. You should

Mark one answer

- ☐ **A.** accelerate to make a gap behind you
- ☐ **B.** touch the brakes sharply to show your brake lights
- ☐ **C.** maintain your speed to prevent the vehicle from overtaking
- ☑ **D.** allow the vehicle to overtake

54 You should ONLY flash your headlights to other road users

Mark one answer

- ☐ **A.** to show that you are giving way
- ☐ **B.** to show that you are about to turn
- ☐ **C.** to tell them that you have right of way
- ☑ **D.** to let them know that you are there

55 At puffin crossings which light will not show to a driver?

Mark one answer

- ☑ **A.** Flashing amber
- ☐ **B.** Red
- ☐ **C.** Steady amber
- ☐ **D.** Green

56 A two-second gap between yourself and the car in front is sufficient when conditions are

Mark one answer

- ☐ **A.** wet
- ☑ **B.** good
- ☐ **C.** damp
- ☐ **D.** foggy

57 You are driving on a clear night. There is a steady stream of oncoming traffic. The national speed limit applies. Which lights should you use?

Mark one answer

- ☐ **A.** Full beam headlights
- ☐ **B.** Sidelights
- ☑ **C.** Dipped headlights
- ☐ **D.** Fog lights

58 You are driving behind a large goods vehicle. It signals left but steers to the right. You should

Mark one answer

- [✓] **A.** slow down and let the vehicle turn
- [ ] **B.** drive on, keeping to the left
- [ ] **C.** overtake on the right of it
- [ ] **D.** hold your speed and sound your horn

59 You are driving along this road. The red van cuts in close in front of you. What should you do?

Mark one answer

- [ ] **A.** Accelerate to get closer to the red van
- [ ] **B.** Give a long blast on the horn
- [✓] **C.** Drop back to leave the correct separation distance
- [ ] **D.** Flash your headlights several times

60 You are waiting in a traffic queue at night. To avoid dazzling following drivers you should

Mark one answer

- [✓] **A.** apply the handbrake only
- [ ] **B.** apply the footbrake only
- [ ] **C.** switch off your headlights
- [ ] **D.** use both the handbrake and footbrake

61 You are driving in traffic at the speed limit for the road. The driver behind is trying to overtake. You should

Mark one answer

- [ ] **A.** move closer to the car ahead, so the driver behind has no room to overtake
- [ ] **B.** wave the driver behind to overtake when it is safe
- [✓] **C.** keep a steady course and allow the driver behind to overtake
- [ ] **D.** accelerate to get away from the driver behind

62 You are driving at night on an unlit road following a slower moving vehicle. You should

Mark one answer

- [ ] **A.** flash your headlights
- [✓] **B.** use dipped beam headlights
- [ ] **C.** switch off your headlights
- [ ] **D.** use full beam headlights

63 A bus lane on your left shows no times of operation. This means it is

Mark one answer

- [ ] **A.** not in operation at all
- [ ] **B.** only in operation at peak times
- [✓] **C.** in operation 24 hours a day
- [ ] **D.** only in operation in daylight hours

54 You are driving along a country road. A horse and rider are approaching. What should you do?

Mark two answers

- A. Increase your speed
- B. Sound your horn
- C. Flash your headlights
- ☑ D. Drive slowly past
- ☑ E. Give plenty of room
- F. Rev your engine

55 A person herding sheep asks you to stop. You should

Mark one answer

- A. ignore them as they have no authority
- ☑ B. stop and switch off your engine
- C. continue on but drive slowly
- D. try and get past quickly

56 When overtaking a horse and rider you should

Mark one answer

- A. sound your horn as a warning
- B. go past as quickly as possible
- C. flash your headlights as a warning
- ☑ D. go past slowly and carefully

57 You are approaching a zebra crossing. Pedestrians are waiting to cross. You should

Mark one answer

- A. give way to the elderly and infirm only
- ☑ B. slow down and prepare to stop
- C. use your headlights to indicate they can cross
- D. wave at them to cross the road

68 You are driving a slow-moving vehicle on a narrow winding road. You should

Mark one answer

- A. keep well out to stop vehicles overtaking dangerously
- B. wave following vehicles past you if you think they can overtake quickly
- ☑ C. pull in safely when you can, to let following vehicles overtake
- D. give a left signal when it is safe for vehicles to overtake you

69 You are driving a slow-moving vehicle on a narrow road. When traffic wishes to overtake you should

Mark one answer

- A. take no action
- B. put your hazard warning lights on
- C. stop immediately and wave it on
- ☑ D. pull in safely as soon as you can do so

70 You are driving a slow-moving vehicle on a narrow winding road. In order to let other vehicles overtake you should

Mark one answer

- A. wave to them to pass
- ☑ B. pull in when you can
- C. show a left turn signal
- D. keep left and hold your speed

71 A vehicle pulls out in front of you at a junction. What should you do?

Mark one answer
- [ ] **A.** Swerve past it and sound your horn
- [ ] **B.** Flash your headlights and drive up close behind
- [x] **C.** Slow down and be ready to stop
- [ ] **D.** Accelerate past it immediately

72 You stop for pedestrians waiting to cross at a zebra crossing. They do not start to cross. What should you do?

Mark one answer
- [x] **A.** Be patient and wait
- [ ] **B.** Sound your horn
- [ ] **C.** Carry on
- [ ] **D.** Wave them to cross

73 You are following this lorry. You should keep well back from it to

Mark one answer
- [x] **A.** give you a good view of the road ahead
- [ ] **B.** stop following traffic from rushing through the junction
- [ ] **C.** prevent traffic behind you from overtaking
- [ ] **D.** allow you to hurry through the traffic lights if they change

74 You are approaching a red light at a puffin crossing. Pedestrians are on the crossing. The red light will stay on until

Mark one answer
- [ ] **A.** you start to edge forward on to the crossing
- [x] **B.** the pedestrians have reached a safe position
- [ ] **C.** the pedestrians are clear of the front of your vehicle
- [ ] **D.** a driver from the opposite direction reach the crossing

75 Which FOUR of these MUST be in good working order for your car to be roadworthy?

Mark four answers

- A. Temperature gauge
- B. Speedometer
- C. Windscreen washers
- D. Windscreen wiper
- E. Oil warning light
- F. Horn

76 New petrol-engined cars must be fitted with catalytic converters. The reason for this is to

Mark one answer

- A. control exhaust noise levels
- B. prolong the life of the exhaust system
- C. allow the exhaust system to be recycled
- D. reduce harmful exhaust emissions

77 What can cause heavy steering?

Mark one answer

- A. Driving on ice
- B. Badly worn brakes
- C. Over-inflated tyres
- D. Under-inflated tyres

78 Driving with under-inflated tyres can affect

Mark two answers

- A. engine temperature
- B. fuel consumption
- C. braking
- D. oil pressure

79 Excessive or uneven tyre wear can be caused by faults in the

Mark two answers

- A. gearbox
- B. braking system
- C. suspension
- D. exhaust system

80 The main cause of brake fade is

Mark one answer

- A. the brakes overheating
- B. air in the brake fluid
- C. oil on the brakes
- D. the brakes out of adjustment

81 Your anti-lock brakes warning light stays on. You should

Mark one answer

- A. check the brake fluid level
- B. check the footbrake free play
- C. check that the handbrake is released
- D. have the brakes checked immediately

82 What does this instrument panel light mean when lit?

Mark one answer

- A. Gear lever in park
- B. Gear lever in neutral
- C. Handbrake on
- D. Handbrake off

83 Which instrument panel warning light would show that headlights are on full beam?

Mark one answer

☑ A.

☐ B.

☐ C.

☐ D.

84 While driving, this warning light on your dashboard comes on. It means

Mark one answer

☑ A. a fault in the braking system

☐ B. the engine oil is low

☐ C. a rear light has failed

☐ D. your seat belt is not fastened

85 You are driving on a motorway. The traffic ahead is braking sharply because of an accident. How could you warn following traffic?

Mark one answer

☑ A. Briefly use the hazard warning lights

☐ B. Switch on the hazard warning lights continuously

☐ C. Briefly use the rear fog lights

☐ D. Switch on the headlights continuously

86 When may you use hazard warning lights?

Mark one answer

☐ A. To park alongside another car

☐ B. To park on double yellow lines

☐ C. When you are being towed

☑ D. When you have broken down

87 Hazard warning lights should be used when vehicles are

Mark one answer

☑ A. broken down and causing an obstruction

☐ B. faulty and moving slowly

☐ C. being towed along a road

☐ D. reversing into a side road

88 It is important to wear suitable shoes when you are driving. Why is this?

Mark one answer

☐ A. To prevent wear on the pedals

☑ B. To maintain control of the pedals

☐ C. To enable you to adjust your seat

☐ D. To enable you to walk for assistance if you break down

89 A properly adjusted head restraint will

Mark one answer

☐ A. make you more comfortable

☑ B. help you to avoid neck injury

☐ C. help you to relax

☐ D. help you to maintain your driving position

90 What will reduce the risk of neck injury resulting from a collision?

Mark one answer

- [ ] **A.** An air-sprung seat
- [ ] **B.** Anti-lock brakes
- [ ] **C.** A collapsible steering wheel
- [ ] **D.** A properly adjusted head restraint

91 You are driving a friend's children home from school. They are both under 14 years old. Who is responsible for making sure they wear a seat belt?

Mark one answer

- [ ] **A.** An adult passenger
- [ ] **B.** The children
- [ ] **C.** You, the driver
- [ ] **D.** Your friend

92 Car passengers MUST wear a seat belt if one is available, unless they are

Mark one answer

- [ ] **A.** under 14 years old
- [ ] **B.** under 1.5 metres (5 feet) in height
- [ ] **C.** sitting in the rear seat
- [x] **D.** exempt for medical reasons

93 You are testing your suspension. You notice that your vehicle keeps bouncing when you press down on the front wing. What does this mean?

Mark one answer

- [ ] **A.** Worn tyres
- [ ] **B.** Tyres under-inflated
- [ ] **C.** Steering wheel not located centrally
- [ ] **D.** Worn shock absorbers

94 You cannot see clearly behind when reversing. What should you do?

Mark one answer

- [ ] **A.** Open your window to look behind
- [ ] **B.** Open the door and look behind
- [ ] **C.** Look in the nearside mirror
- [x] **D.** Ask someone to guide you

95 When driving a car fitted with automatic transmission what would you use 'kick down' for?

Mark one answer

- [ ] **A.** Cruise control
- [x] **B.** Quick acceleration
- [ ] **C.** Slow braking
- [ ] **D.** Fuel economy

96 A roof rack fitted to your car will

Mark one answer

- [ ] **A.** reduce fuel consumption
- [ ] **B.** improve the road handling
- [ ] **C.** make your car go faster
- [x] **D.** increase fuel consumption

97 It is illegal to drive with tyres that

Mark one answer

- [ ] **A.** have been bought second-hand
- [x] **B.** have a large deep cut in the side wall
- [ ] **C.** are of different makes
- [ ] **D.** are of different tread patterns

98 The legal minimum depth of tread for car tyres over three-quarters of the breadth is

Mark one answer

- A. 1mm
- ☑ B. 1.6mm
- C. 2.5mm
- D. 4mm

99 You are carrying two 13 year old children and their parents in your car. Who is responsible for seeing that the children wear seat belts?

Mark one answer

- A. The children's parents
- ☑ B. You, the driver
- C. The front-seat passenger
- D. The children

100 When a roof rack is not in use it should be removed. Why is this?

Mark one answer

- A. It will affect the suspension
- B. It is illegal
- C. It will affect your braking
- ☑ D. It will waste fuel

101 You have a loose filler cap on your diesel fuel tank. This will

Mark two answers

- ☑ A. waste fuel and money
- ☑ B. make roads slippery for other road users
- C. improve your vehicle's fuel consumption
- D. increase the level of exhaust emissions

102 How can you, as a driver, help the environment?

Mark three answers

- ☑ A. By reducing your speed
- ☑ B. By gentle acceleration
- C. By using leaded fuel
- D. By driving faster
- E. By harsh acceleration
- ☑ F. By servicing your vehicle properly

103 To help the environment, you can avoid wasting fuel by

Mark three answers

- ☑ A. having your vehicle properly serviced
- ☑ B. making sure your tyres are correctly inflated
- ☑ C. not over-revving in the lower gears
- D. driving at higher speeds where possible
- E. keeping an empty roof rack properly fitted
- F. servicing your vehicle less regularly

104 To reduce the volume of traffic on the roads you could

Mark three answers

- ☑ A. use public transport more often
- ☑ B. share a car when possible
- ☑ C. walk or cycle on short journeys
- D. travel by car at all times
- E. use a car with a smaller engine
- F. drive in a bus lane

105 Which THREE of the following are most likely to waste fuel?

Mark three answers

- [ ] **A.** Reducing your speed
- [x] **B.** Carrying unnecessary weight
- [ ] **C.** Using the wrong grade of fuel
- [x] **D.** Under-inflated tyres
- [ ] **E.** Using different brands of fuel
- [x] **F.** A fitted, empty roof rack

106 To avoid spillage after refuelling, you should make sure that

Mark one answer

- [ ] **A.** your tank is only ¾ full
- [ ] **B.** you have used a locking filler cap
- [ ] **C.** you check your fuel gauge is working
- [x] **D.** your filler cap is securely fastened

107 Which THREE things can you, as a road user, do to help the environment?

Mark three answers

- [x] **A.** Cycle when possible
- [ ] **B.** Drive on under-inflated tyres
- [ ] **C.** Use the choke for as long as possible on a cold engine
- [x] **D.** Have your vehicle properly tuned and serviced
- [x] **E.** Watch the traffic and plan ahead
- [ ] **F.** Brake as late as possible without skidding

108 As a driver you can cause MORE damage to the environment by

Mark three answers

- [ ] **A.** choosing a fuel-efficient vehicle
- [x] **B.** making a lot of short journeys
- [ ] **C.** driving in as high a gear as possible
- [x] **D.** accelerating as quickly as possible
- [ ] **E.** having your vehicle regularly serviced
- [x] **F.** using leaded fuel

109 Extra care should be taken when refuelling, because diesel fuel when spilt is

Mark one answer

- [ ] **A.** sticky
- [ ] **B.** odourless
- [ ] **C.** clear
- [x] **D.** slippery

110 To help protect the environment you should NOT

Mark one answer

- [ ] **A.** remove your roof rack when unloaded
- [x] **B.** use your car for very short journeys
- [ ] **C.** walk, cycle, or use public transport
- [ ] **D.** empty the boot of unnecessary weight

111 Daytime visibility is poor but not seriously reduced. You should switch on

Mark one answer

- [ ] **A.** headlights and fog lights
- [ ] **B.** front fog lights
- [x] **C.** dipped headlights
- [ ] **D.** rear fog lights

112 Why are vehicles fitted with rear fog lights?

Mark one answer

- A. To be seen when driving at high speed
- B. To use if broken down in a dangerous position
- ☑ C. To make them more visible in thick fog
- D. To warn drivers following closely to drop back

113 Which THREE does the law require you to keep in good condition?

Mark three answers

- A. Gears
- B. Transmission
- ☑ C. Headlights
- ☑ D. Windscreen
- ☑ E. Seat belts

114 Driving at 70mph uses more fuel than driving at 50mph by up to

Mark one answer

- A. 10%
- ☑ B. 30%
- C. 75%
- D. 100%

115 Your vehicle pulls to one side when braking. You should

Mark one answer

- A. change the tyres around
- ☑ B. consult your garage as soon as possible
- C. pump the pedal when braking
- D. use your handbrake at the same time

116 As a driver you can help reduce pollution levels in town centres by

Mark one answer

- A. driving more quickly
- B. using leaded fuel
- ☑ C. walking or cycling
- D. driving short journeys

117 Unbalanced wheels on a car may cause

Mark one answer

- A. the steering to pull to one side
- ☑ B. the steering to vibrate
- C. the brakes to fail
- D. the tyres to deflate

118 Turning the steering wheel while your car is stationary can cause damage to the

Mark two answers

- A. gearbox
- B. engine
- C. brakes
- ☑ D. steering
- ☑ E. tyres

119 How can you reduce the chances of your car being broken into when leaving it unattended?

Mark one answer

- ☑ A. Take all contents with you
- B. Park near a taxi rank
- C. Place any valuables on the floor
- D. Park near a fire station

120 You have to leave valuables in your car. It would be safer to

Mark one answer
- A. put them in a carrier bag
- B. park near a school entrance
- C. lock them out of sight ✓
- D. park near a bus stop

121 How could you deter theft from your car when leaving it unattended?

Mark one answer
- A. Leave valuables in a carrier bag
- B. Lock valuables out of sight ✓
- C. Put valuables on the seats
- D. Leave valuables on the floor

122 Which of the following may help to deter a thief from stealing your car?

Mark one answer
- A. Always keeping the headlights on
- B. Fitting reflective glass windows
- C. Always keeping the interior light on
- D. Etching the car number on the windows ✓

123 How can you help to prevent your car radio being stolen?

Mark one answer
- A. Park in an unlit area
- B. Hide the radio with a blanket
- C. Park near a busy junction
- D. Install a security-coded radio ✓

124 Which of the following should not be kept in your vehicle?

Mark one answer
- A. A first aid kit
- B. A road atlas
- C. The tax disc
- D. The vehicle documents ✓

125 What should you do when leaving your vehicle?

Mark one answer
- A. Put valuable documents under the seats
- B. Remove all valuables ✓
- C. Cover valuables with a blanket
- D. Leave the interior light on

126 You are parking your car. You have some valuables which you are unable to take with you. What should you do?

Mark one answer
- A. Park near a police station
- B. Put them under the driver's seat
- C. Lock them out of sight ✓
- D. Park in an unlit side road

127 Which of these is most likely to deter the theft of your vehicle?

Mark one answer
- A. An immobiliser ✓
- B. Tinted windows
- C. Locking wheel nuts
- D. A sun screen

128 Wherever possible, which one of the following should you do when parking at night?

Mark one answer

- A. Park in a quiet car park
- ☑ B. Park in a well-lit area
- C. Park facing against the flow of traffic
- D. Park next to a busy junction

129 When parking and leaving your car you should

Mark one answer

- A. park under a shady tree
- B. remove the tax disc
- C. park in a quiet road
- ☑ D. engage the steering lock

130 Rear-facing baby seats should NEVER be used on a seat protected with

Mark one answer

- ☑ A. an airbag
- B. seat belts
- C. head restraints
- D. seat covers

131 When leaving your vehicle parked and unattended you should

Mark one answer

- A. park near a busy junction
- B. park in a housing estate
- ☑ C. remove the key and lock it
- D. leave the left indicator on

132 How can you lessen the risk of your vehicle being broken into at night?

Mark one answer

- ☑ A. Leave it in a well lit area
- B. Park in a quiet side road
- C. Don't engage the steering lock
- D. Park in a poorly lit area

133 To help keep your car secure you could join a

Mark one answer

- A. vehicle breakdown organisation
- ☑ B. vehicle watch scheme
- C. advanced drivers' scheme
- D. car maintenance class

134 Which TWO of the following will improve fuel consumption?

Mark two answers

- ☑ A. Reducing your road speed
- ☑ B. Planning well ahead
- C. Late and harsh braking
- D. Driving in lower gears
- E. Short journeys with a cold engine
- F. Rapid acceleration

135 You service your own vehicle. How should you get rid of the old engine oil?

Mark one answer

- ☑ A. Take it to a local authority site
- B. Pour it down a drain
- C. Tip it into a hole in the ground
- D. Put it into your dustbin

136 On your vehicle, where would you find a catalytic converter?

Mark one answer

- ☐ A. In the fuel tank
- ☐ B. In the air filter
- ☐ C. On the cooling system
- ☑ D. On the exhaust system

137 Why do MOT tests include a strict exhaust emission test?

Mark one answer

- ☐ A. To recover the cost of expensive garage equipment
- ☑ B. To help protect the environment against pollution
- ☐ C. To discover which fuel supplier is used the most
- ☐ D. To make sure diesel and petrol engines emit the same fumes

138 To reduce the damage your vehicle causes to the environment you should

Mark three answers

- ☐ A. use narrow side streets
- ☑ B. avoid harsh acceleration
- ☑ C. brake in good time
- ☑ D. anticipate well ahead
- ☐ E. use busy routes

139 Your vehicle has a catalytic converter. Its purpose is to reduce

Mark one answer

- ☐ A. exhaust noise
- ☐ B. fuel consumption
- ☑ C. exhaust emissions
- ☐ D. engine noise

140 For which TWO of these may you use hazard warning lights?

Mark two answers

- ☑ A. When driving on a motorway to warn drivers behind of a hazard ahead
- ☐ B. When you are double-parked on a two-way road
- ☐ C. When your direction indicators are not working
- ☐ D. When warning oncoming traffic that you intend to stop
- ☑ E. When your vehicle has broken down and is causing an obstruction

141 A properly serviced vehicle will give

Mark two answers

- ☐ A. lower insurance premiums
- ☐ B. you a refund on your road tax
- ☑ C. better fuel economy
- ☑ D. cleaner exhaust emissions

142 You enter a road where there are road humps. What should you do?

Mark one answer

- ☑ A. Maintain a reduced speed throughout
- ☐ B. Accelerate quickly between each one
- ☐ C. Always keep to the maximum legal speed
- ☐ D. Drive slowly at school times only

143 When should you especially check the engine oil level?

Mark one answer

- ☑ **A.** Before a long journey
- ☐ **B.** When the engine is hot
- ☐ **C.** Early in the morning
- ☐ **D.** Every 6000 miles

144 Which of these, if allowed to get low, could cause an accident?

Mark one answer

- ☐ **A.** Antifreeze level
- ☑ **B.** Brake fluid level
- ☐ **C.** Battery water level
- ☐ **D.** Radiator coolant level

145 Which TWO are badly affected if the tyres are under-inflated?

Mark two answers

- ☑ **A.** Braking
- ☑ **B.** Steering
- ☐ **C.** Changing gear
- ☐ **D.** Parking

146 When MUST you use dipped headlights during the day?

Mark one answer

- ☐ **A.** All the time
- ☐ **B.** Along narrow streets
- ☑ **C.** In poor visibility
- ☐ **D.** When parking

147 Motor vehicles can harm the environment. This has resulted in

Mark three answers

- ☑ **A.** air pollution
- ☑ **B.** damage to buildings
- ☐ **C.** reduced health risks
- ☐ **D.** improved public transport
- ☐ **E.** less use of electrical vehicles
- ☑ **F.** using up natural resources

148 Excessive or uneven tyre wear can be caused by faults in which THREE?

Mark three answers

- ☐ **A.** The gearbox
- ☑ **B.** The braking system
- ☐ **C.** The accelerator
- ☐ **D.** The exhaust system
- ☑ **E.** Wheel alignment
- ☑ **F.** The suspension

149 You must NOT sound your horn

Mark one answer

- ☐ **A.** between 10pm and 6am in a built-up area
- ☐ **B.** at any time in a built-up area
- ☑ **C.** between 11.30pm and 7am in a built-up area
- ☐ **D.** between 11.30pm and 6am on any road

150 The pictured vehicle is 'environmentally friendly' because it

Mark three answers

- ☑ **A.** reduces noise pollution
- ☐ **B.** uses diesel fuel
- ☑ **C.** uses electricity
- ☐ **D.** uses unleaded fuel
- ☐ **E.** reduces parking spaces
- ☑ **F.** reduces town traffic

151 Supertrams or Light Rapid Transit (LRT) systems are environmentally friendly because

Mark one answer

- ☐ **A.** they use diesel power
- ☐ **B.** they use quieter roads
- ☑ **C.** they use electric power
- ☐ **D.** they do not operate during rush hour

152 'Red routes' in major cities have been introduced to

Mark one answer

- ☐ **A.** raise the speed limits
- ☑ **B.** help the traffic flow
- ☐ **C.** provide better parking
- ☐ **D.** allow lorries to load more freely

153 In some narrow residential streets you will find a speed limit of

Mark one answer

- ☑ **A.** 20mph
- ☐ **B.** 25mph
- ☐ **C.** 35mph
- ☐ **D.** 40mph

154 Road humps, chicanes, and narrowings are

Mark one answer

- ☐ **A.** always at major road works
- ☐ **B.** used to increase traffic speed
- ☐ **C.** at toll-bridge approaches only
- ☑ **D.** traffic calming measures

155 The purpose of a catalytic converter is to reduce

Mark one answer

- ☐ **A.** fuel consumption
- ☐ **B.** the risk of fire
- ☑ **C.** toxic exhaust gases
- ☐ **D.** engine wear

156 It is essential that tyre pressures are checked regularly. When should this be done?

Mark one answer

- ☐ **A.** After any lengthy journey
- ☐ **B.** After travelling at high speed
- ☐ **C.** When tyres are hot
- ☑ **D.** When tyres are cold

157 When should you NOT use your horn in a built-up area?

Mark one answer
- A. Between 8pm and 8am
- B. Between 9pm and dawn
- C. Between dusk and 8am
- ☑ D. Between 11.30pm and 7am

158 Why are mirrors often slightly curved (convex)?

Mark one answer
- ☑ A. They give a wider field of vision
- B. They totally cover blind spots
- C. They make it easier to judge the speed of following traffic
- D. They make following traffic look bigger

159 Catalytic converters are fitted to make the

Mark one answer
- A. engine produce more power
- B. exhaust system easier to replace
- C. engine run quietly
- ☑ D. exhaust fumes cleaner

160 You will use more fuel if your tyres are

Mark one answer
- ☑ A. under-inflated
- B. of different makes
- C. over-inflated
- D. new and hardly used

161 For which TWO of these may you use hazard warning lights?

Mark two answers
- ☑ A. When travelling on a motorway, to warn drivers behind of a hazard ahead
- B. When you are double-parked on a two-way road
- C. When your direction indicators are not working
- D. When warning oncoming traffic that you intend to stop
- ☑ E. When your vehicle has broken down and is causing an obstruction

162 How should you dispose of a used battery?

Mark two answers
- ☑ A. Take it to a local authority site
- B. Put it in the dustbin
- C. Break it up into pieces
- D. Leave it on waste land
- ☑ E. Take it to a garage
- F. Burn it on a fire

163 What is most likely to cause high fuel consumption?

Mark one answer
- A. Poor steering control
- B. Accelerating around bends
- C. Staying in high gears
- ☑ D. Harsh braking and accelerating

164 Braking distances on ice can be

Mark one answer

- A. twice the normal distance
- B. five times the normal distance
- C. seven times the normal distance
- D. ten times the normal distance

165 Freezing conditions will affect the distance it takes you to come to a stop. You should expect stopping distances to increase by up to

Mark one answer

- A. two times
- B. three times
- C. five times
- D. ten times

166 In very hot weather the road surface can get soft. Which TWO of the following will be affected most?

Mark two answers

- A. The suspension
- B. The grip of the tyres
- C. The braking
- D. The exhaust

167 Where are you most likely to be affected by a sidewind?

Mark one answer

- A. On a narrow country lane
- B. On an open stretch of road
- C. On a busy stretch of road
- D. On a long, straight road

168 In windy conditions you need to take extra care when

Mark one answer

- A. using the brakes
- B. making a hill start
- C. turning into a narrow road
- D. passing pedal cyclists ✓

169 What is the shortest stopping distance at 70mph?

Mark one answer

- A. 53 metres (175 feet)
- B. 60 metres (197 feet)
- C. 73 metres (240 feet)
- D. 96 metres (315 feet) ✓

170 What is the shortest overall stopping distance on a dry road from 60mph?

Mark one answer

- A. 53 metres (175 feet)
- B. 58 metres (190 feet)
- C. 73 metres (240 feet) ✓
- D. 96 metres (315 feet)

171 Your indicators may be difficult to see in bright sunlight. What should you do?

Mark one answer

- A. Put your indicator on earlier
- B. Give an arm signal as well as using your indicator ✓
- C. Touch the brake several times to show the stop lights
- D. Turn as quickly as you can

172 In very hot weather the road surface can get soft. Which TWO of the following will be affected most?

Mark two answers
- A. The suspension
- ☑ B. The steering
- ☑ C. The braking
- D. The exhaust

173 When approaching a right-hand bend you should keep well to the left. Why is this?

Mark one answer
- ☑ A. To improve your view of the road
- B. To overcome the effect of the road's slope
- C. To let faster traffic from behind overtake
- D. To be positioned safely if you skid

174 You should not overtake when

Mark three answers
- ☑ A. intending to turn left shortly afterwards
- B. in a one-way street
- ☑ C. approaching a junction
- D. going up a long hill
- ☑ E. the view ahead is blocked

175 You have just gone through deep water. To dry off the brakes you should

Mark one answer
- A. accelerate and keep to a high speed for short time
- ☑ B. go slowly while gently applying the brakes
- C. avoid using the brakes at all for a few miles
- D. stop for at least an hour to allow them time to dry

176 You are on a fast, open road in good conditions. For safety, the distance between you and the veh in front should be

Mark one answer
- ☑ A. a two-second time gap
- B. one car length
- C. 2 metres (6 feet 6 inches)
- D. two car lengths

177 What is the most common cause o skidding?

Mark one answer
- A. Worn tyres
- ☑ B. Driver error
- C. Other vehicles
- D. Pedestrians

178 You are driving on an icy road. How can you avoid wheelspin?

Mark one answer

- A. Drive at a slow speed in as high a gear as possible
- B. Use the handbrake if the wheels start to slip
- C. Brake gently and repeatedly
- D. Drive in a low gear at all times

179 Skidding is mainly caused by

Mark one answer

- A. the weather
- B. the driver
- C. the vehicle
- D. the road

180 You are driving in freezing conditions. What should you do when approaching a sharp bend?

Mark two answers

- A. Slow down before you reach the bend
- B. Gently apply your handbrake
- C. Firmly use your footbrake
- D. Coast into the bend
- E. Avoid sudden steering movements

181 You are turning left on a slippery road. The back of your vehicle slides to the right. You should

Mark one answer

- A. brake firmly and not turn the steering wheel
- B. steer carefully to the left
- C. steer carefully to the right
- D. brake firmly and steer to the left

182 You are braking on a wet road. Your vehicle begins to skid. Your vehicle does not have anti-lock brakes. What is the FIRST thing you should do?

Mark one answer

- A. Quickly pull up the handbrake
- B. Release the footbrake fully ✓
- C. Push harder on the brake pedal
- D. Gently use the accelerator

183 Coasting the vehicle

Mark one answer

- A. improves the driver's control
- B. makes steering easier
- C. reduces the driver's control ✓
- D. uses more fuel

184 Before starting a journey in freezing weather you should clear ice and snow from your vehicle's

Mark four answers

- A. aerial
- B. windows ✓
- C. bumper
- D. lights ✓
- E. mirrors ✓
- F. number plates ✓

185 You are trying to move off on snow. You should use

Mark one answer

- A. the lowest gear you can
- B. the highest gear you can ✓
- C. a high engine speed
- D. the handbrake and footbrake together

186 When driving in falling snow you should

Mark one answer

- A. brake firmly and quickly
- B. be ready to steer sharply
- C. use sidelights only
- ☑ D. brake gently in plenty of time

187 The main benefit of having four-wheel drive is to improve

Mark one answer

- ☑ A. road holding
- B. fuel consumption
- C. stopping distances
- D. passenger comfort

188 When driving in fog in daylight you should use

Mark one answer

- A. sidelights
- B. full beam headlights
- C. hazard lights
- ☑ D. dipped headlights

189 You are about to go down a steep hill. To control the speed of your vehicle you should

Mark one answer

- A. select a high gear and use the brakes carefully
- B. select a high gear and use the brakes firmly
- ☑ C. select a low gear and use the brakes carefully
- D. select a low gear and avoid using the brakes

190 How can you use the engine of you vehicle as a brake?

Mark one answer

- ☑ A. By changing to a lower gear
- B. By selecting reverse gear
- C. By changing to a higher gear
- D. By selecting neutral gear

191 You wish to park facing DOWNHILL Which TWO of the following shoul you do?

Mark two answers

- ☑ A. Turn the steering wheel towards the ker
- B. Park close to the bumper of another car
- C. Park with two wheels on the kerb
- ☑ D. Put the handbrake on firmly
- E. Turn the steering wheel away from the k

192 You are driving in a built-up area. approach a speed hump. You shoul

Mark one answer

- A. move across to the left-hand side of the road
- B. wait for any pedestrians to cross
- ☑ C. slow your vehicle right down
- D. stop and check both pavements

193 You are on a long, downhill slope. What should you do to help control the speed of your vehicle?

Mark one answer

- A. Select neutral
- ☑ B. Select a lower gear
- C. Grip the handbrake firmly
- D. Apply the parking brake gently

194 Your vehicle is fitted with anti-lock brakes. To stop quickly in an emergency you should

Mark one answer

- A. brake firmly and pump the brake pedal on and off
- ☑ B. brake rapidly and firmly without releasing the brake pedal
- C. brake gently and pump the brake pedal on and off
- D. brake rapidly once, and immediately release the brake pedal

195 Anti-lock brakes prevent wheels from locking. This means the tyres are less likely to

Mark one answer

- A. aquaplane
- ☑ B. skid
- C. puncture
- D. wear

196 Anti-lock brakes reduce the chances of a skid occurring particularly when

Mark one answer

- A. driving down steep hills
- B. braking during normal driving
- ☑ C. braking in an emergency
- D. driving on good road surfaces

197 Anti-lock brakes are most effective when you

Mark one answer

- A. keep pumping the foot brake to prevent skidding
- B. brake normally, but grip the steering wheel tightly
- ☑ C. brake rapidly and firmly until you have slowed down
- D. apply the handbrake to reduce the stopping distance

198 Your car is fitted with anti-lock brakes. You need to stop in an emergency. You should

Mark one answer

- A. brake normally and avoid turning the steering wheel
- ☑ B. press the brake pedal rapidly and firmly until you have stopped
- C. keep pushing and releasing the foot brake quickly to prevent skidding
- D. apply the handbrake to reduce the stopping distance

199 Vehicles fitted with anti-lock brakes

Mark one answer

- A. are impossible to skid
- ☑ B. can be steered while you are braking
- C. accelerate much faster
- D. are not fitted with a handbrake

200 Anti-lock brakes may not work as effectively if the road surface is

Mark two answers

- [ ] A. dry
- [x] B. loose
- [x] C. wet
- [ ] D. good
- [ ] E. firm

201 Anti-lock brakes are of most use when you are

Mark one answer

- [ ] A. braking gently
- [ ] B. driving on worn tyres
- [x] C. braking excessively
- [ ] D. driving normally

202 Driving a vehicle fitted with anti-lock brakes allows you to

Mark one answer

- [ ] A. brake harder because it is impossible to skid
- [ ] B. drive at higher speeds
- [x] C. steer and brake at the same time
- [ ] D. pay less attention to the road ahead

203 Anti-lock brakes can greatly assist with

Mark one answer

- [ ] A. a higher cruising speed
- [x] B. steering control when braking
- [ ] C. control when accelerating
- [ ] D. motorway driving

204 When would an anti-lock braking system start to work?

Mark one answer

- [ ] A. After the parking brake has been applied
- [ ] B. Whenever pressure on the brake pedal is applied
- [x] C. Just as the wheels are about to lock
- [ ] D. When the normal braking system fails to operate

205 You are driving a vehicle fitted with anti-lock brakes. You need to stop in an emergency. You should apply the footbrake

Mark one answer

- [ ] A. slowly and gently
- [ ] B. slowly but firmly
- [ ] C. rapidly and gently
- [x] D. rapidly and firmly

206 Your vehicle has anti-lock brakes, but they may not always prevent skidding. This is most likely to happen when driving

Mark two answers

- [ ] A. in foggy conditions
- [x] B. on surface water
- [x] C. on loose road surfaces
- [ ] D. on dry tarmac
- [ ] E. at night on unlit roads

207 Anti-lock brakes will take effect when

Mark one answer

- [ ] **A.** you do not brake quickly enough
- [x] **B.** excessive brake pressure has been applied
- [ ] **C.** you have not seen a hazard ahead
- [ ] **D.** speeding on slippery road surfaces

208 When driving in fog, which of the following are correct?

Mark three answers

- [x] **A.** Use dipped headlights
- [ ] **B.** Use headlights on full beam
- [x] **C.** Allow more time for your journey
- [ ] **D.** Keep close to the car in front
- [x] **E.** Slow down
- [ ] **F.** Use sidelights only

209 You are driving along a country road. You see this sign. AFTER dealing safely with the hazard you should always

Mark one answer

- [ ] **A.** check your tyre pressures
- [ ] **B.** switch on your hazard warning lights
- [ ] **C.** accelerate briskly
- [x] **D.** test your brakes

210 You are driving in falling snow. Your wipers are not clearing the windscreen. You should

Mark one answer

- [ ] **A.** set the windscreen demister to cool
- [x] **B.** be prepared to clear the windscreen by hand
- [ ] **C.** use the windscreen washers
- [ ] **D.** partly open the front windows

211 You are driving in heavy rain. Your steering suddenly becomes very light. You should

Mark one answer

- [ ] **A.** steer towards the side of the road
- [ ] **B.** apply gentle acceleration
- [ ] **C.** brake firmly to reduce speed
- [x] **D.** ease off the accelerator

212 How can you tell when you are driving over black ice?

Mark one answer

- [ ] **A.** It is easier to brake
- [ ] **B.** The noise from your tyres sounds louder
- [ ] **C.** You see black ice on the road
- [x] **D.** Your steering feels light

213 The roads are icy. You should drive slowly

Mark one answer

- [x] **A.** in the highest gear possible
- [ ] **B.** in the lowest gear possible
- [ ] **C.** with the handbrake partly on
- [ ] **D.** with your left foot on the brake

214 You are driving along a wet road. How can you tell if your vehicle is aquaplaning?

Mark one answer
- [ ] A. The engine will stall
- [ ] B. The engine noise will increase
- [ ] C. The steering will feel very heavy
- [x] D. The steering will feel very light

215 How can you tell if you are driving on ice?

Mark two answers
- [ ] A. The tyres make a rumbling noise
- [x] B. The tyres make hardly any noise
- [ ] C. The steering becomes heavier
- [x] D. The steering becomes lighter

216 You are driving along a wet road. How can you tell if your vehicle's tyres are losing their grip on the surface?

Mark one answer
- [ ] A. The engine will stall
- [ ] B. The steering will feel very heavy
- [ ] C. The engine noise will increase
- [x] D. The steering will feel very light

217 You are travelling at 50mph on a good, dry road. What is your shortest overall stopping distance?

Mark one answer
- [ ] A. 36 metres (120 feet)
- [x] B. 53 metres (175 feet)
- [ ] C. 75 metres (245 feet)
- [ ] D. 96 metres (315 feet)

218 Your overall stopping distance will be much longer when driving

Mark one answer
- [x] A. in the rain
- [ ] B. in fog
- [ ] C. at night
- [ ] D. in strong winds

219 You have driven through a flood. What is the first thing you should do?

Mark one answer
- [ ] A. Stop and check the tyres
- [ ] B. Stop and dry the brakes
- [ ] C. Check your exhaust
- [x] D. Test your brakes

220 You are on a good, dry road surface and your vehicle has good brakes and tyres. What is the overall stopping distance at 40mph?

Mark one answer
- [ ] A. 23 metres (75 feet)
- [x] B. 36 metres (118 feet)
- [ ] C. 53 metres (175 feet)
- [ ] D. 96 metres (315 feet)

221 You are on a good, dry road surface. Your vehicle has good brakes and tyres. What is the BRAKING distance at 50mph?

Mark one answer
- [x] A. 38 metres (125 feet)
- [ ] B. 14 metres (46 feet)
- [ ] C. 24 metres (79 feet)
- [ ] D. 55 metres (180 feet)

222 What does the solid white line at the side of the road indicate?

Mark one answer

- [ ] **A.** Traffic lights ahead
- [✓] **B.** Edge of the carriageway
- [ ] **C.** Footpath on the left
- [ ] **D.** Cycle path

224 You are driving along this motorway. It is raining. When following this lorry you should

Mark two answers

- [ ] **A.** allow at least a two-second gap
- [ ] **B.** move left and drive on the hard shoulder
- [✓] **C.** allow at least a four-second gap
- [✓] **D.** be aware of spray reducing your vision
- [ ] **E.** move right and stay in the right hand lane

223 You are driving towards this level crossing. What would be the first warning of an approaching train?

Mark one answer

- [ ] **A.** Both half barriers down
- [✓] **B.** A steady amber light
- [ ] **C.** One half barrier down
- [ ] **D.** Twin flashing red lights

225 You are behind this cyclist. When the traffic lights change, what should you do?

Mark one answer

- [ ] **A.** Try to move off before the cyclist
- [✓] **B.** Allow the cyclist time and room
- [ ] **C.** Turn right but give the cyclist room
- [ ] **D.** Tap your horn and drive through first

226

You are driving towards this left-hand bend. What dangers should you be aware of?

Mark one answer

- [ ] **A.** A vehicle overtaking you
- [ ] **B.** No white lines in the centre of the road
- [ ] **C.** No sign to warn you of the bend
- [✓] **D.** Pedestrians walking towards you

227

While driving, you see this sign ahead. You should

Mark one answer

- [ ] **A.** stop at the sign
- [✓] **B.** slow, but continue around the bend
- [ ] **C.** slow to a crawl and continue
- [ ] **D.** stop and look for open farm gates

228

Why should the junction on the left be kept clear?

Mark one answer

- [✓] **A.** To allow vehicles to enter and emerge
- [ ] **B.** To allow the bus to reverse
- [ ] **C.** To allow vehicles to make a 'U' turn
- [ ] **D.** To allow vehicles to park

229

When the traffic lights change to green the white car should

Mark one answer

- [✓] **A.** wait for the cyclist to pull away
- [ ] **B.** move off quickly and turn in front of the cyclist
- [ ] **C.** move close up to the cyclist to beat the lights
- [ ] **D.** sound the horn to warn the cyclist

230 You intend to turn left at the traffic lights. Just before turning you should

Mark one answer
- [ ] **A.** check your right mirror
- [ ] **B.** move close up to the white car
- [ ] **C.** straddle the lanes
- [x] **D.** check for bicycles on your left

231 You should reduce your speed when driving along this road because

Mark one answer
- [x] **A.** there is a staggered junction ahead
- [ ] **B.** there is a low bridge ahead
- [ ] **C.** there is a change in the road surface
- [ ] **D.** the road ahead narrows

232 You are driving at 60mph. As you approach this hazard you should

Mark one answer
- [ ] **A.** maintain your speed
- [x] **B.** reduce your speed
- [ ] **C.** take the next right turn
- [ ] **D.** take the next left turn

233 The traffic ahead of you in the left lane is slowing. You should

Mark two answers
- [x] **A.** be wary of cars on your right cutting in
- [ ] **B.** accelerate past the vehicles in the left lane
- [ ] **C.** pull up on the left-hand verge
- [ ] **D.** move across and continue in the right-hand lane
- [x] **E.** slow down keeping a safe separation distance

234 What might you expect to happen in this situation?

Mark one answer

- **A.** Traffic will move into the right-hand lane
- ☑ **B.** Traffic speed will increase
- ☑ **C.** Traffic will move into the left-hand lane
- **D.** Traffic will not need to change position

235 You are driving on a road with several lanes. You see these signs above the lanes. What do they mean?

Mark one answer

- **A.** The two right lanes are open
- ☑ **B.** The two left lanes are open
- **C.** Traffic in the left lanes should stop
- **D.** Traffic in the right lanes should stop

236 As a provisional licence holder, you must not drive a motor car

Mark two answers

- **A.** at more than 50mph
- ☑ **B.** on your own
- ☑ **C.** on the motorway
- **D.** under the age of 18 years at night
- **E.** with passengers in the rear seats

237 After passing your driving test, you suffer from ill health. This affects your driving. You MUST

Mark one answer

- **A.** inform your local police station
- **B.** get on as best you can
- **C.** not inform anyone as you hold a full licence
- ☑ **D.** inform the licensing authority

238 You are invited to a pub lunch. You know that you will have to drive in the evening. What is your best cours of action?

Mark one answer

- **A.** Avoid mixing your alcoholic drinks
- ☑ **B.** Not drink any alcohol at all
- **C.** Have some milk before drinking alcohol
- **D.** Eat a hot meal with your alcoholic drinks

239 You have been convicted of driving whilst unfit through drink or drugs. You will find this is likely to cause the cost of one of the following to rise considerably. Which one?

Mark one answer

- **A.** Road fund licence
- ☑ **B.** Insurance premiums
- **C.** Vehicle test certificate
- **D.** Driving licence

240 What advice should you give to a driver who has had a few alcoholic drinks at a party?

Mark one answer

- A. Have a strong cup of coffee and then drive home
- B. Drive home carefully and slowly
- C. Go home by public transport
- D. Wait a short while and then drive home

241 You have been taking medicine for a few days which made you feel drowsy. Today you feel better but still need to take the medicine. You should only drive

Mark one answer

- A. if your journey is necessary
- B. at night on quiet roads
- C. if someone goes with you
- D. after checking with your doctor

242 You are about to return home from holiday when you become ill. A doctor prescribes drugs which are likely to affect your driving. You should

Mark one answer

- A. drive only if someone is with you
- B. avoid driving on motorways
- C. not drive yourself
- D. never drive at more than 30mph

243 During periods of illness your ability to drive may be impaired. You MUST

Mark two answers

- A. see your doctor each time before you drive
- B. only take smaller doses of any medicines
- ☑ C. be medically fit to drive
- ☑ D. not drive after taking certain medicines
- E. take all your medicines with you when you drive

244 You feel drowsy when driving. You should

Mark two answers

- ☑ A. stop and rest as soon as possible
- B. turn the heater up to keep you warm and comfortable
- ☑ C. make sure you have a good supply of fresh air
- D. continue with your journey but drive more slowly
- E. close the car windows to help you concentrate

245 You are driving along a motorway and become tired. You should

Mark two answers

- ☑ A. stop at the next service area and rest
- ☑ B. leave the motorway at the next exit and rest
- C. increase your speed and turn up the radio volume
- D. close all your windows and set heating to warm
- E. pull up on the hard shoulder and change drivers

246 You are taking drugs that are likely to affect your driving. What should you do?

Mark one answer

- ☑ **A.** Seek medical advice before driving
- ☐ **B.** Limit your driving to essential journeys
- ☐ **C.** Only drive if accompanied by a full licence-holder
- ☐ **D.** Drive only for short distances

247 You are about to drive home. You feel very tired and have a severe headache. You should

Mark one answer

- ☑ **A.** wait until you are fit and well before driving
- ☐ **B.** drive home, but take a tablet for headaches
- ☐ **C.** drive home if you can stay awake for the journey
- ☐ **D.** wait for a short time, then drive home slowly

248 If you are feeling tired it is best to stop as soon as you can. Until then you should

Mark one answer

- ☐ **A.** increase your speed to find a stopping place quickly
- ☑ **B.** ensure a supply of fresh air
- ☐ **C.** gently tap the steering wheel
- ☐ **D.** keep changing speed to improve concentration

249 If your motorway journey seems boring and you feel drowsy whilst driving you should

Mark one answer

- ☑ **A.** open a window and drive to the next service area
- ☐ **B.** stop on the hard shoulder for a sleep
- ☐ **C.** speed up to arrive at your destination sooner
- ☐ **D.** slow down and let other drivers overtake

250 Driving long distances can be tiring. You can prevent this by

Mark three answers

- ☑ **A.** stopping every so often for a walk
- ☑ **B.** opening a window for some fresh air
- ☑ **C.** ensuring plenty of refreshment breaks
- ☐ **D.** completing the journey without stopping
- ☐ **E.** eating a large meal before driving

251 You go to a social event and need to drive a short time after. What precaution should you take?

Mark one answer

- ☐ **A.** Avoid drinking alcohol on an empty stomach
- ☐ **B.** Drink plenty of coffee after drinking alcohol
- ☑ **C.** Avoid drinking alcohol completely
- ☐ **D.** Drink plenty of milk before drinking alcohol

252 You take some cough medicine given to you by a friend. What should you do before driving?

Mark one answer

- **A.** Ask your friend if taking the medicine affected their driving
- **B.** Drink some strong coffee one hour before driving
- **C.** Check the label to see if the medicine will affect your driving
- **D.** Drive a short distance to see if the medicine is affecting your driving

253 You take the wrong route and find you are on a one-way street. You should

Mark one answer

- **A.** reverse out of the road
- **B.** turn round in a side road
- **C.** continue to the end of the road
- **D.** reverse into a driveway

254 Which THREE are likely to make you lose concentration while driving?

Mark three answers

- **A.** Looking at road maps
- **B.** Listening to loud music
- **C.** Using your windscreen washers
- **D.** Looking in your wing mirror
- **E.** Using a mobile phone

255 You are driving along this road. The driver on the left is reversing from a driveway. You should

Mark one answer

- **A.** move to the opposite side of the road
- **B.** drive through as you have priority
- **C.** sound your horn and be prepared to stop ✓
- **D.** speed up and drive through quickly

256 You have been involved in an argument before starting your journey. This has made you feel angry. You should

Mark one answer

- **A.** start to drive, but open a window
- **B.** drive slower than normal and turn your radio on
- **C.** have an alcoholic drink to help you relax before driving
- **D.** calm down before you start to drive ✓

257 You start to feel tired while driving. What should you do?

Mark one answer

- **A.** Increase your speed slightly
- **B.** Decrease your speed slightly
- **C.** Find a less busy route
- **D.** Pull over at a safe place to rest ✓

258
You are driving on this dual carriageway. Why may you need to slow down?

Mark one answer

- A. There is a broken white line in the centre
- B. There are solid white lines either side
- ☑ C. There are roadworks ahead of you
- D. There are no footpaths

259
You have just been overtaken by this motorcyclist who is cutting in sharply. You should

Mark one answer

- A. sound the horn
- B. brake firmly
- ☑ C. keep a safe gap
- D. flash your lights

260
You are about to drive home. You cannot find the glasses you need to wear. You should

Mark one answer

- A. drive home slowly, keeping to quiet roads
- B. borrow a friend's glasses and use those
- C. drive home at night, so that the lights will help you
- ☑ D. find a way of getting home without driving

261
Which THREE result from drinking alcohol ?

Mark three answers

- ☑ A. Less control
- ☑ B. A false sense of confidence
- C. Faster reactions
- ☑ D. Poor judgement of speed
- E. Greater awareness of danger

262
Which THREE of these are likely effects of drinking alcohol?

Mark three answers

- ☑ A. Reduced coordination
- ☑ B. Increased confidence
- ☑ C. Poor judgement
- D. Increased concentration
- E. Faster reactions
- F. Colour blindness

263
How does alcohol affect you?

Mark one answer

- A. It speeds up your reactions
- B. It increases your awareness
- C. It improves your coordination
- ☑ D. It reduces your concentration

264 Your doctor has given you a course of medicine. Why should you ask how it will affect you?

Mark one answer

- [ ] **A.** Drugs make you a better driver by quickening your reactions
- [ ] **B.** You will have to let your insurance company know about the medicine
- [✓] **C.** Some types of medicine can cause your reactions to slow down
- [ ] **D.** The medicine you take may affect your hearing

265 You are not sure if your cough medicine will affect you. What TWO things could you do?

Mark two answers

- [✓] **A.** Ask your doctor
- [✓] **B.** Check the medicine label
- [ ] **C.** Drive if you feel alright
- [ ] **D.** Ask a friend or relative for advice

266 You are on a motorway. You feel tired. You should

Mark one answer

- [ ] **A.** carry on but go slowly
- [✓] **B.** leave the motorway at the next exit
- [ ] **C.** complete your journey as quickly as possible
- [ ] **D.** stop on the hard shoulder

267 You find that you need glasses to read vehicle number plates at the required distance. When MUST you wear them?

Mark one answer

- [ ] **A.** Only in bad weather conditions
- [✓] **B.** At all times when driving
- [ ] **C.** Only when you think it necessary
- [ ] **D.** Only in bad light or at night time

268 Which TWO things would help to keep you alert during a long journey?

Mark two answers

- [ ] **A.** Finishing your journey as fast as you can
- [ ] **B.** Keeping off the motorways and using country roads
- [✓] **C.** Making sure that you get plenty of fresh air
- [✓] **D.** Making regular stops for refreshments

269 Which of the following types of glasses should NOT be worn when driving at night?

Mark one answer

- [ ] **A.** Half-moon
- [ ] **B.** Round
- [ ] **C.** Bi-focal
- [✓] **D.** Tinted

270 Drinking any amount of alcohol is likely to

Mark three answers

- ☑ **A.** slow down your reactions to hazards
- ☐ **B.** increase the speed of your reactions
- ☑ **C.** worsen your judgement of speed
- ☐ **D.** improve your awareness of danger
- ☑ **E.** give a false sense of confidence

271 What else can seriously affect your concentration, other than alcoholic drinks?

Mark three answers

- ☑ **A.** Drugs
- ☑ **B.** Tiredness
- ☐ **C.** Tinted windows
- ☐ **D.** Contact lenses
- ☑ **E.** Loud music

272 As a driver you find that your eyesight has become very poor. Your optician says they cannot help you. The law says that you should tell

Mark one answer

- ☑ **A.** the licensing authority
- ☐ **B.** your own doctor
- ☐ **C.** the local police station
- ☐ **D.** another optician

273 You see this sign on the rear of a slow-moving lorry that you want to pass. It is travelling in the middle lane of a three lane motorway. You should

Mark one answer

- ☐ **A.** cautiously approach the lorry then pass on either side
- ☐ **B.** follow the lorry until you can leave the motorway
- ☐ **C.** wait on the hard shoulder until the lorry has stopped
- ☑ **D.** approach with care and keep to the left of the lorry

274 Where would you expect to see these markers?

Mark two answers

- A. On a motorway sign
- B. At the entrance to a narrow bridge
- ☑ C. On a large goods vehicle
- ☑ D. On a builder's skip placed on the road

275 What does this signal from a police officer, mean to oncoming traffic?

Mark one answer

- A. Go ahead
- ☑ B. Stop
- C. Turn left
- D. Turn right

276 What is the main hazard shown in this picture?

Mark one answer

- A. Vehicles turning right
- B. Vehicles doing U-turns
- ☑ C. The cyclist crossing the road
- D. Parked cars around the corner

277 Which road user has caused a hazard?

Mark one answer

- ☑ A. The parked car (arrowed A)
- B. The pedestrian waiting to cross (arrowed B)
- C. The moving car (arrowed C)
- D. The car turning (arrowed D)

278
What should the driver of the car approaching the crossing do?

Mark one answer

- A. Continue at the same speed
- B. Sound the horn
- C. Drive through quickly
- ☑ D. Slow down and get ready to stop

279
What should the driver of the red car (arrowed) do?

Mark one answer

- A. Wave the pedestrians who are waiting to cross
- ☑ B. Wait for the pedestrian in the road to cross
- C. Quickly drive behind the pedestrian in the road
- D. Tell the pedestrian in the road she should not have crossed

280
What THREE things should the driver of the grey car (arrowed) be especially aware of?

Mark three answers

- ☑ A. Pedestrians stepping out between cars
- B. Other cars behind the grey car
- ☑ C. Doors opening on parked cars
- D. The bumpy road surface
- ☑ E. Cars leaving parking spaces
- F. Empty parking spaces

281
What should the driver of the red car (arrowed) do?

Mark one answer

- A. Sound the horn to tell other drivers where he is
- B. Squeeze through the gap
- C. Wave the driver of the white car to go on
- ☑ D. Wait until the car blocking the way has moved

282 What should the driver of the grey car (arrowed) do?

Mark one answer

A. Cross if the way is clear
B. Reverse out of the box junction
C. Wait in the same place until the lights are green
D. Wait until the lights are red then cross

283 The driver of which car has caused a hazard?

Mark one answer

A. Car A
B. Car B
C. Car C
D. Car D

284 You think the driver of the vehicle in front has forgotten to cancel the right indicator. You should

Mark one answer

A. flash your lights to alert the driver
B. sound your horn before overtaking
C. overtake on the left if there is room
D. stay behind and not overtake

285 What is the main hazard the driver of the red car (arrowed) should be most aware of?

Mark one answer

A. Glare from the sun may affect the driver's vision
B. The black car may stop suddenly
C. The bus may move out into the road
D. Oncoming vehicles will assume the driver is turning right

286 In heavy motorway traffic you are being followed closely by the vehicle behind. How can you lower the risk of an accident?

Mark one answer
- ☑ **A.** Increase your distance from the vehicle in front
- ☐ **B.** Tap your foot on the brake pedal sharply
- ☐ **C.** Switch on your hazard lights
- ☐ **D.** Move onto the hard shoulder and stop

287 You see this sign ahead. You should expect the road to

Mark one answer
- ☐ **A.** go steeply uphill
- ☐ **B.** go steeply downhill
- ☑ **C.** bend sharply to the left
- ☐ **D.** bend sharply to the right

288 You are approaching this cyclist. You should

Mark one answer
- ☐ **A.** overtake before the cyclist gets to the junction
- ☐ **B.** flash your headlights at the cyclist
- ☑ **C.** slow down and allow the cyclist to turn
- ☐ **D.** overtake the cyclist on the left-hand side

289 Why must you take extra care when turning right at this junction?

Mark one answer
- ☐ **A.** Road surface is poor
- ☐ **B.** Footpaths are narrow
- ☐ **C.** Road markings are faint
- ☑ **D.** There is reduced visibility

290 This yellow sign on a vehicle indicates this is

Mark one answer

- **A.** a vehicle broken down
- **B.** a school bus ✓
- **C.** an ice cream van
- **D.** a private ambulance

291 When approaching this bridge you should give way to

Mark one answer

- **A.** bicycles
- **B.** buses ✓
- **C.** motorcycles
- **D.** cars

292 What type of vehicle could you expect to meet in the middle of the road?

Mark one answer

- **A.** Lorry ✓
- **B.** Bicycle
- **C.** Car
- **D.** Motorcycle

293 At this blind junction you must stop

Mark one answer

- **A.** behind the line, then edge forward to see clearly ✓
- **B.** beyond the line at a point where you can see clearly
- **C.** only if there is traffic on the main road
- **D.** only if you are turning to the right

294 A driver pulls out of a side road in front of you. You have to brake hard. You should

Mark one answer

- [x] **A.** ignore the error and stay calm
- [ ] **B.** flash your lights to show your annoyance
- [ ] **C.** sound your horn to show your annoyance
- [ ] **D.** overtake as soon as possible

295 An elderly person's driving ability could be affected because they may be unable to

Mark one answer

- [ ] **A.** obtain car insurance
- [ ] **B.** understand road signs
- [x] **C.** react very quickly
- [ ] **D.** give signals correctly

296 You have just passed these warning lights. What hazard would you expect to see next?

Mark one answer

- [ ] **A.** A level crossing with no barrier
- [ ] **B.** An ambulance station
- [x] **C.** A school crossing patrol
- [ ] **D.** An opening bridge

297 Why should you be especially cautious when going past this bus?

Mark two answers

- [ ] **A.** There is traffic approaching in the distance
- [ ] **B.** The driver may open the door
- [x] **C.** It may suddenly move off
- [x] **D.** People may cross the road in front of it
- [ ] **E.** There are bicycles parked on the pavement

298 In areas where there are 'traffic calming' measures you should

Mark one answer

- [x] **A.** drive at a reduced speed
- [ ] **B.** always drive at the speed limit
- [ ] **C.** position your vehicle in the centre of the road
- [ ] **D.** only slow down if pedestrians are near

299 You are planning a long journey. Do you need to plan rest stops?

Mark one answer

- ☐ **A.** Yes, you should plan to stop every half an hour
- ☐ **B.** Yes, regular stops help concentration
- ☐ **C.** No, you will be less tired if you get there as soon as possible
- ☐ **D.** No, only fuel stops will be needed

300 A driver does something that upsets you. You should

Mark one answer

- ☐ **A.** try not to react
- ☐ **B.** let them know how you feel
- ☐ **C.** flash your headlights several times
- ☐ **D.** sound your horn

301 The red lights are flashing. What should you do when approaching this level crossing ?

Mark one answer

- ☐ **A.** Go through quickly
- ☐ **B.** Go through carefully
- ☑ **C.** Stop before the barrier
- ☐ **D.** Switch on hazard warning lights

302 What are TWO main hazards you should be aware of when going along this street?

Mark two answers

- ☐ **A.** Glare from the sun
- ☑ **B.** Car doors opening suddenly
- ☐ **C.** Lack of road markings
- ☐ **D.** The headlights on parked cars being switched on
- ☐ **E.** Large goods vehicles
- ☑ **F.** Children running out from between vehicles

303 What is the main hazard you should be aware of when following this cyclist?

Mark one answer

- ☐ **A.** The cyclist may move into the left and dismount
- ☑ **B.** The cyclist may swerve out into the road
- ☐ **C.** The contents of the cyclist's carrier may fall onto the road
- ☐ **D.** The cyclist may wish to turn right at the end of the road

304
When approaching this hazard why should you slow down?

Mark two answers

- [✓] **A.** Because of the bend
- [ ] **B.** Because it's hard to see to the right
- [ ] **C.** Because of approaching traffic
- [ ] **D.** Because of animals crossing
- [✓] **E.** Because of the level crossing

305
A driver's behaviour has upset you. may help if you

Mark one answer

- [✓] **A.** stop and take a break
- [ ] **B.** shout abusive language
- [ ] **C.** gesture to them with your hand
- [ ] **D.** follow their car, flashing the headlights

306 You want to reverse into a side road. You are not sure that the area behind your car is clear. What should you do?

Mark one answer

- A. Look through the rear window only
- B. Get out and check
- C. Check the mirrors only
- D. Carry on, assuming it is clear

307 You are about to reverse into a side road. A pedestrian wishes to cross behind you. You should

Mark one answer

- A. wave to the pedestrian to stop
- B. give way to the pedestrian
- C. wave to the pedestrian to cross
- D. reverse before the pedestrian starts to cross

308 Who is especially in danger of not being seen as you reverse your car?

Mark one answer

- A. Motorcyclists
- B. Car drivers
- C. Cyclists
- D. Children

309 You are reversing around a corner when you notice a pedestrian walking behind you. What should you do?

Mark one answer

- A. Slow down and wave the pedestrian across
- B. Continue reversing and steer round the pedestrian
- C. Stop and give way
- D. Continue reversing and sound your horn

310 You want to turn right from a junction but your view is restricted by parked vehicles. What should you do?

Mark one answer

- A. Move out quickly, but be prepared to stop
- B. Sound your horn and pull out if there is no reply
- C. Stop, then move slowly forward until you have a clear view
- D. Stop, get out and look along the main road to check

311 You are at the front of a queue of traffic waiting to turn right into a side road. Why is it important to check your right mirror just before turning?

Mark one answer

- A. To look for pedestrians about to cross
- B. To check for overtaking vehicles
- C. To make sure the side road is clear
- D. To check for emerging traffic

312
In which THREE places would parking your vehicle cause danger or obstruction to other road users?

Mark three answers
- ☑ **A.** In front of a property entrance
- ☑ **B.** At or near a bus stop
- ☐ **C.** On your driveway
- ☐ **D.** In a marked parking space
- ☑ **E.** On the approach to a level crossing

313
In which THREE places would parking cause an obstruction to others?

Mark three answers
- ☑ **A.** Near the brow of a hill
- ☐ **B.** In a lay-by
- ☐ **C.** Where the kerb is raised
- ☑ **D.** Where the kerb has been lowered for wheelchairs
- ☑ **E.** At or near a bus stop

314
What must a driver do at a pelican crossing when the amber light is flashing?

Mark one answer
- ☐ **A.** Signal the pedestrian to cross
- ☐ **B.** Always wait for the green light before proceeding
- ☑ **C.** Give way to any pedestrians on the crossing
- ☐ **D.** Wait for the red-and-amber light before proceeding

315
You have stopped at a pelican crossing. A disabled person is crossing slowly in front of you. The lights have now changed to green. You should

Mark two answers
- ☑ **A.** allow the person to cross
- ☐ **B.** drive in front of the person
- ☐ **C.** drive behind the person
- ☐ **D.** sound your horn
- ☑ **E.** be patient
- ☐ **F.** edge forward slowly

316
You are driving past parked cars. You notice a wheel of a bicycle sticking out between them. What should you do?

Mark one answer
- ☐ **A.** Accelerate past quickly and sound your horn
- ☐ **B.** Slow down and wave the cyclist across
- ☐ **C.** Brake sharply and flash your headlights
- ☑ **D.** Slow down and be prepared to stop for a cyclist

317 You are driving past a line of parked cars. You notice a ball bouncing out into the road ahead. What should you do?

Mark one answer

- [ ] **A.** Continue driving at the same speed and sound your horn
- [ ] **B.** Continue driving at the same speed and flash your headlights
- [✓] **C.** Slow down and be prepared to stop for children
- [ ] **D.** Stop and wave the children across to fetch their ball

318 You want to turn right from a main road into a side road. Just before turning you should

Mark one answer

- [ ] **A.** cancel your right-turn signal
- [ ] **B.** select first gear
- [✓] **C.** check for traffic overtaking on your right
- [ ] **D.** stop and set the handbrake

319 You are driving in slow-moving queues of traffic. Just before changing lane you should

Mark one answer

- [ ] **A.** sound the horn
- [✓] **B.** look for motorcyclists filtering through the traffic
- [ ] **C.** give a 'slowing down' arm signal
- [ ] **D.** change down to first gear

320 You are driving in town. There is a bus at the bus stop on the other side of the road. Why should you be careful?

Mark one answer

- [ ] **A.** The bus may have broken down
- [✓] **B.** Pedestrians may come from behind the bus
- [ ] **C.** The bus may move off suddenly
- [ ] **D.** The bus may remain stationary

321 How should you overtake horse riders?

Mark one answer

- [ ] **A.** Drive up close and overtake as soon as possible
- [ ] **B.** Speed is not important but allow plenty of room
- [ ] **C.** Use your horn just once to warn them
- [✓] **D.** Drive slowly and leave plenty of room

322 A friend wants to teach you to drive a car. They must

Mark one answer

- A. be over 21 and have held a full licence for at least two years
- B. be over 18 and hold an advanced driver's certificate
- C. be over 18 and have fully comprehensive insurance
- ☑ D. be over 21 and have held a full licence for at least three years

323 You are dazzled at night by a vehicle behind you. You should

Mark one answer

- ☑ A. set your mirror to anti-dazzle
- B. set your mirror to dazzle the other driver
- C. brake sharply to a stop
- D. switch your rear lights on and off

324 You have a collision whilst your car is moving. What is the first thing you must do?

Mark one answer

- A. Stop only if there are injured people
- B. Call the emergency services
- ☑ C. Stop at the scene of the accident
- D. Call your insurance company

325 Yellow zig zag lines on the road outside schools mean

Mark one answer

- A. sound your horn to alert other road users
- B. stop to allow children to cross
- ☑ C. you must not wait or park on these lines
- D. you must not drive over these lines

326 What do these road markings outside a school mean?

Mark one answer

- A. You may park here if you are a teacher
- B. Sound your horn before parking
- C. When parking use your hazard warning lights
- ☑ D. You must not wait or park your vehicle here

327 You are driving on a main road. You intend to turn right into a side road. Just before turning you should

Mark one answer

- **A.** adjust your interior mirror
- **B.** flash your headlamps
- **C.** steer over to the left
- ✓ **D.** check for traffic overtaking on your right

328 Why should you allow extra room when overtaking a motorcyclist on a windy day?

Mark one answer

- **A.** The rider may turn off suddenly to get out of the wind
- ✓ **B.** The rider may be blown across in front of you
- **C.** The rider may stop suddenly
- **D.** The rider may be travelling faster than normal

329 Which age group of drivers is most likely to be involved in a road accident?

Mark one answer

- **A.** 36 to 45-year-olds
- **B.** 55-year-olds and over
- **C.** 46 to 55-year-olds
- ✓ **D.** 17 to 25-year-olds

330 The road outside this school is marked with yellow zig zag lines. What do these lines mean?

Mark one answer

- **A.** You may park on the lines when dropping off school children
- **B.** You may park on the lines when picking school children up
- ✓ **C.** You must not wait or park your vehicle here at all
- **D.** You must stay with your vehicle if you park here

331 You are driving towards a zebra crossing. Waiting to cross is a person in a wheelchair. You should

Mark one answer

- **A.** continue on your way
- **B.** wave to the person to cross
- **C.** wave to the person to wait
- ✓ **D.** be prepared to stop

332 Where in particular should you look out for motorcyclists?

Mark one answer
- [ ] **A.** In a filling station
- [√] **B.** At a road junction
- [ ] **C.** Near a service area
- [ ] **D.** When entering a car park

333 Where should you take particular care to look out for motorcyclists and cyclists?

Mark one answer
- [ ] **A.** On dual carriageways
- [√] **B.** At junctions
- [ ] **C.** At zebra crossings
- [ ] **D.** On one-way streets

334 Which sign means that there may be people walking along the road?

Mark one answer
- [ ] **A.**
- [ ] **B.**
- [ ] **C.**
- [√] **D.**

335 You are turning left at a junction. Pedestrians have started to cross the road. You should

Mark one answer
- [ ] **A.** go on, giving them plenty of room
- [ ] **B.** stop and wave at them to cross
- [ ] **C.** blow your horn and proceed
- [√] **D.** give way to them

336 You are turning left from a main road into a side road. People are already crossing the road into which you are turning. You should

Mark one answer
- [ ] **A.** continue, as it is your right of way
- [ ] **B.** signal to them to continue crossing
- [√] **C.** wait and allow them to cross
- [ ] **D.** sound your horn to warn them of your presence

337 You are at a road junction, turning into a minor road. There are pedestrians crossing the minor road. You should

rk one answer

A. stop and wave the pedestrians across

B. sound your horn to let the pedestrians know that you are there

C. give way to the pedestrians who are already crossing

D. carry on; the pedestrians should give way to you

---

338 You are turning left into a side road. What hazards should you be especially aware of?

rk one answer

A. One way street

B. Pedestrians

C. Traffic congestion

D. Parked vehicles

---

339 You intend to turn right into a side road. Just before turning you should check for motorcyclists who might be

rk one answer

A. overtaking on your left

B. following you closely

C. emerging from the side road

D. overtaking on your right

---

340 A toucan crossing is different from other crossings because

Mark one answer

A. moped riders can use it

B. it is controlled by a traffic warden

C. it is controlled by two flashing lights

☑ D. cyclists can use it

---

341 At toucan crossings

Mark two answers

A. there is no flashing amber light

B. cyclists are not permitted

C. there is a continuously flashing amber beacon

☑ D. pedestrians and cyclists may cross

E. you only stop if someone is waiting to cross

---

342 What does this sign tell you?

Mark one answer

A. No cycling

☑ B. Cycle route ahead

C. Route for cycles only

D. End of cycle route

343 How will a school crossing patrol signal you to stop?

Mark one answer

- A. By pointing to children on the opposite pavement
- B. By displaying a red light
- [✓] C. By displaying a stop sign
- D. By giving you an arm signal

344 Where would you see this sign?

Mark one answer

- A. In the window of a car taking children to school
- B. At the side of the road
- C. At playground areas
- [✓] D. On the rear of a school bus or coach

345 Which sign tells you that pedestrians may be walking in the road as there is no pavement?

Mark one answer

[✓] A.

B.

C.

D.

346 What does this sign mean?

Mark one answer

- A. No route for pedestrians and cyclists
- B. A route for pedestrians only
- C. A route for cyclists only
- [✓] D. A route for pedestrians and cyclists

347 You see a pedestrian with a white stick and red band. This means that the person is

Mark one answer

- A. physically disabled
- B. deaf only
- C. blind only
- [✓] D. deaf and blind

348 What action would you take when elderly people are crossing the road?

rk one answer
- [ ] **A.** Wave them across so they know that you have seen them
- [ ] **B.** Be patient and allow them to cross in their own time
- [ ] **C.** Rev the engine to let them know that you are waiting
- [ ] **D.** Tap the horn in case they are hard of hearing

349 You see two elderly pedestrians about to cross the road ahead. You should

rk one answer
- [ ] **A.** expect them to wait for you to pass
- [ ] **B.** speed up to get past them quickly
- [ ] **C.** stop and wave them across the road
- [ ] **D.** be careful, they may misjudge your speed

350 What does this sign mean?

Mark one answer
- [ ] **A.** Contra-flow pedal cycle lane
- [✓] **B.** With-flow pedal cycle lane
- [ ] **C.** Pedal cycles and buses only
- [ ] **D.** No pedal cycles or buses

351 You should NEVER attempt to overtake a cyclist

Mark one answer
- [✓] **A.** just before you turn left
- [ ] **B.** just before you turn right
- [ ] **C.** on a one-way street
- [ ] **D.** on a dual carriageway

352 You are coming up to a roundabout. A cyclist is signalling to turn right. What should you do?

Mark one answer
- [ ] **A.** Overtake on the right
- [ ] **B.** Give a horn warning
- [ ] **C.** Signal the cyclist to move across
- [✓] **D.** Give the cyclist plenty of room

353

You are approaching this roundabout and see the cyclist signal right. Why is the cyclist keeping to the left?

Mark one answer

- [ ] **A.** It is a quicker route for the cyclist
- [ ] **B.** The cyclist is going to turn left instead
- [ ] **C.** The cyclist thinks *The Highway Code* does not apply to bicycles
- [✓] **D.** The cyclist is slower and more vulnerable

354

When you are overtaking a cyclist you should leave as much room as you would give to a car. What is the main reason for this?

Mark one answer

- [ ] **A.** The cyclist might change lanes
- [ ] **B.** The cyclist might get off the bike
- [✓] **C.** The cyclist might swerve
- [ ] **D.** The cyclist might have to make a right turn

355

Which TWO should you allow extra room when overtaking?

Mark two answers

- [✓] **A.** Motorcycles
- [ ] **B.** Tractors
- [✓] **C.** Bicycles
- [ ] **D.** Road-sweeping vehicles

356

Why should you look particularly f motorcyclists and cyclists at junctions?

Mark one answer

- [ ] **A.** They may want to turn into the side roa
- [ ] **B.** They may slow down to let you turn
- [✓] **C.** They are harder to see
- [ ] **D.** They might not see you turn

357

You are waiting to come out of a s road. Why should you watch caref for motorcycles?

Mark one answer

- [ ] **A.** Motorcycles are usually faster than cars
- [ ] **B.** Police patrols often use motorcycles
- [✓] **C.** Motorcycles are small and hard to see
- [ ] **D.** Motorcycles have right of way

358

In daylight, an approaching motorcyclist is using a dipped headlight. Why?

Mark one answer

- [✓] **A.** So that the rider can be seen more easil
- [ ] **B.** To stop the battery overcharging
- [ ] **C.** To improve the rider's vision
- [ ] **D.** The rider is inviting you to proceed

359

Motorcyclists should wear bright clothing mainly because

Mark one answer

- [ ] **A.** they must do so by law
- [ ] **B.** it helps keep them cool in summer
- [ ] **C.** the colours are popular
- [✓] **D.** drivers often do not see them

360 There is a slow-moving motorcyclist ahead of you. You are unsure what the rider is going to do. You should

Mark one answer

- A. pass on the left
- B. pass on the right
- ☑ C. stay behind
- D. move closer

361 Motorcyclists will often look round over their right shoulder just before turning right. This is because

Mark one answer

- A. they need to listen for following traffic
- B. motorcycles do not have mirrors
- C. looking around helps them balance as they turn
- ☑ D. they need to check for traffic in their blind area

362 At road junctions which of the following are most vulnerable?

Mark three answers

- ☑ A. Cyclists
- ☑ B. Motorcyclists
- ☑ C. Pedestrians
- D. Car drivers
- E. Lorry drivers

363 Motorcyclists are particularly vulnerable

Mark one answer

- A. when moving off
- B. on dual carriageways
- ☑ C. when approaching junctions
- D. on motorways

364 Ahead of you there is a vehicle with a flashing amber beacon. This means it is

Mark one answer

- ☑ A. slow moving
- B. broken down
- C. a doctor's car
- D. a school crossing patrol

365 An injured motorcyclist is lying unconscious in the road. You should

Mark one answer

- A. remove the safety helmet
- ☑ B. seek medical assistance
- C. move the person off the road
- D. remove the leather jacket

366 You notice horse riders in front. What should you do FIRST?

Mark one answer

- A. Pull out to the middle of the road
- ☑ B. Be prepared to slow down
- C. Accelerate around them
- D. Signal right

367 You are approaching a roundabout. There are horses just ahead of you. You should

Mark two answers
- ☑ **A.** be prepared to stop
- ☐ **B.** treat them like any other vehicle
- ☑ **C.** give them plenty of room
- ☐ **D.** accelerate past as quickly as possible
- ☐ **E.** sound your horn as a warning

368 Which THREE should you do when passing sheep on a road?

Mark three answers
- ☑ **A.** Allow plenty of room
- ☑ **B.** Go very slowly
- ☐ **C.** Pass quickly but quietly
- ☑ **D.** Be ready to stop
- ☐ **E.** Briefly sound your horn

369 At night you see a pedestrian wearing reflective clothing and carrying a bright red light. What does this mean?

Mark one answer
- ☐ **A.** You are approaching roadworks
- ☑ **B.** You are approaching an organised walk
- ☐ **C.** You are approaching a slow-moving vehicle
- ☐ **D.** You are approaching an accident black spot

370 As you approach a pelican crossing the lights change to green. Elderly people are halfway across. You shou

Mark one answer
- ☐ **A.** wave them to cross as quickly as they can
- ☐ **B.** rev your engine to make them hurry
- ☐ **C.** flash your lights in case they have not heard you
- ☑ **D.** wait because they will take longer to cros

371 There are flashing amber lights und a school warning sign. What action should you take?

Mark one answer
- ☑ **A.** Reduce speed until you are clear of the are
- ☐ **B.** Keep up your speed and sound the horn
- ☐ **C.** Increase your speed to clear the area quick
- ☐ **D.** Wait at the lights until they change to green

372 Which of the following types of crossing can detect when people ar on them?

Mark one answer
- ☐ **A.** Pelican
- ☐ **B.** Toucan
- ☐ **C.** Zebra
- ☑ **D.** Puffin

373 You are approaching this crossing. You should

Mark one answer
- ☑ **A.** prepare to slow down and stop
- ☐ **B.** stop and wave the pedestrians across
- ☐ **C.** speed up and pass by quickly
- ☐ **D.** drive on unless the pedestrians step out

374 You see a pedestrian with a dog. The dog has a bright orange lead and collar. This especially warns you that the pedestrian is

Mark one answer
- ☐ **A.** elderly
- ☐ **B.** dog training
- ☐ **C.** colour blind
- ☑ **D.** deaf

375 These road markings must be kept clear to allow

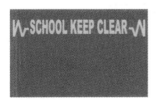

Mark one answer
- ☐ **A.** school children to be dropped off
- ☐ **B.** for teachers to park
- ☐ **C.** school children to be picked up
- ☑ **D.** a clear view of the crossing area

376 You must not stop on these road markings because you may obstruct

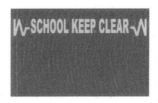

Mark one answer
- ☑ **A.** children's view of the crossing area
- ☐ **B.** teachers' access to the school
- ☐ **C.** delivery vehicles' access to the school
- ☐ **D.** emergency vehicles' access to the school

377 The left-hand pavement is closed due to street repairs. What should you do?

Mark one answer
- ☑ **A.** Watch out for pedestrians walking in the road
- ☐ **B.** Use your right-hand mirror more often
- ☐ **C.** Speed up to get past the road works quicker
- ☐ **D.** Position your vehicle close to the left-hand kerb

378 Stopping on these road markings may obstruct

Mark one answer

- [ ] **A.** emergency vehicles' access to the school
- [✓] **B.** drivers' view of the crossing area
- [ ] **C.** teachers' access to the school
- [ ] **D.** delivery vehicles' access to the school

379 Where would you see this sign?

Mark one answer

- [ ] **A.** Near a school crossing
- [ ] **B.** At a playground entrance
- [✓] **C.** On a school bus
- [ ] **D.** At a 'pedestrians only' area

380 You are following a motorcyclist on an uneven road. You should

Mark one answer

- [ ] **A.** allow less room so you can be seen in their mirrors
- [ ] **B.** overtake immediately
- [✓] **C.** allow extra room in case they swerve to avoid pot-holes
- [ ] **D.** allow the same room as normal because road surfaces do not affect motorcyclists

381 You are following two cyclists. They approach a roundabout in the left-hand lane. In which direction should you expect the cyclists to go

Mark one answer

- [ ] **A.** Left
- [ ] **B.** Right
- [✓] **C.** Any direction
- [ ] **D.** Straight ahead

382 You are travelling behind a moped. You want to turn left just ahead. You should

Mark one answer

- [ ] **A.** overtake the moped before the junction
- [ ] **B.** pull alongside the moped and stay level until just before the junction
- [ ] **C.** sound your horn as a warning and pull in front of the moped
- [✓] **D.** stay behind until the moped has passed the junction

383 Which THREE of the following are hazards motorcyclists present in queues of traffic?

Mark three answers

- [✓] **A.** Cutting in just in front of you
- [ ] **B.** Riding in single file
- [✓] **C.** Passing very close to you
- [ ] **D.** Riding with their headlight on dipped beam
- [✓] **E.** Filtering between the lanes

384

You see a horse rider as you approach a roundabout. They are signalling right but keeping well to the left. You should

Mark one answer

- A. proceed as normal
- B. keep close to them
- C. cut in front of them
- ✓ D. stay well back

385

How would you react to drivers who appear to be inexperienced?

Mark one answer

- A. Sound your horn to warn them of your presence
- ✓ B. Be patient and prepare for them to react more slowly
- C. Flash your headlights to indicate that it is safe for them to proceed
- D. Overtake them as soon as possible

386

You are following a learner driver who stalls at a junction. You should

Mark one answer

- ✓ A. be patient as you expect them to make mistakes
- B. stay very close behind and flash your headlights
- C. start to rev your engine if they take too long to restart
- D. immediately steer around them and drive on

387

You are on a country road. What should you expect to see coming towards you on YOUR side of the road?

Mark one answer

- A. Motorcycles
- B. Bicycles
- ✓ C. Pedestrians
- D. Horse riders

388

You are turning left into a side road. Pedestrians are crossing the road near the junction. You must

Mark one answer

- A. wave them on
- B. sound your horn
- C. switch on your hazard lights
- ✓ D. wait for them to cross

389 You are following a car driven by an elderly driver. You should

Mark one answer

- [ ] **A.** expect the driver to drive badly
- [ ] **B.** flash your lights and overtake
- [✓] **C.** be aware that the driver's reactions may not be as fast as yours
- [ ] **D.** stay very close behind but be careful

390 You are following a cyclist. You wish to turn left just ahead. You should

Mark one answer

- [ ] **A.** overtake the cyclist before the junction
- [ ] **B.** pull alongside the cyclist and stay level until after the junction
- [✓] **C.** hold back until the cyclist has passed the junction
- [ ] **D.** go around the cyclist on the junction

391 A horse rider is in the left-hand lane approaching a roundabout. You should expect the rider to

Mark one answer

- [✓] **A.** go in any direction
- [ ] **B.** turn right
- [ ] **C.** turn left
- [ ] **D.** go ahead

392 You have just passed your test. How can you decrease your risk of accidents on the motorway?

Mark one answer

- [ ] **A.** By keeping up with the car in front
- [ ] **B.** By never going over 40mph
- [ ] **C.** By staying only in the left-hand lane
- [✓] **D.** By taking further training

393

The road is wet. Why might a motorcyclist steer round drain covers on a bend?

Mark one answer

- A. To avoid puncturing the tyres on the edge of the drain covers
- ☑ B. To prevent the motorcycle sliding on the metal drain covers
- C. To help judge the bend using the drain covers as marker points
- D. To avoid splashing pedestrians on the pavement

394

You are about to overtake a slow-moving motorcyclist. Which one of these signs would make you take special care?

Mark one answer

☑ A.

B.

C.

D.

395

You are waiting to emerge left from a minor road. A large vehicle is approaching from the right. You have time to turn, but you should wait. Why?

Mark one answer

- ☑ A. The large vehicle can easily hide an overtaking vehicle
- B. The large vehicle can turn suddenly
- C. The large vehicle is difficult to steer in a straight line
- D. The large vehicle can easily hide vehicles from the left

396

You are following a long vehicle. It approaches a crossroads and signals left, but moves out to the right. You should

Mark one answer

- A. get closer in order to pass it quickly
- ☑ B. stay well back and give it room
- C. assume the signal is wrong and it is really turning right
- D. overtake as it starts to slow down

397 You are following a long vehicle approaching a crossroads. The driver signals right but moves close to the left-hand kerb. What should you do?

Mark one answer

- A. Warn the driver of the wrong signal
- ☑ B. Wait behind the long vehicle
- C. Report the driver to the police
- D. Overtake on the right-hand side

398 You are approaching a mini-roundabout. The long vehicle in front is signalling left but positioned over to the right. You should

Mark one answer

- A. sound your horn
- B. overtake on the left
- C. follow the same course as the lorry
- ☑ D. keep well back

399 Before overtaking a large vehicle you should keep well back. Why is this?

Mark one answer

- A. To give acceleration space to overtake quickly on blind bends
- ☑ B. To get the best view of the road ahead
- C. To leave a gap in case the vehicle stops and rolls back
- D. To offer other drivers a safe gap if they want to overtake you

400 You wish to overtake a long, slow-moving vehicle on a busy road. You should

Mark one answer

- A. follow it closely and keep moving out to see the road ahead
- B. flash your headlights for the oncoming traffic to give way
- C. stay behind until the driver waves you past
- ☑ D. keep well back until you can see that it is clear

401 Why is passing a lorry more risky than passing a car?

Mark one answer

- ☑ A. Lorries are longer than cars
- B. Lorries may suddenly pull up
- C. The brakes of lorries are not as good
- D. Lorries climb hills more slowly

402 You are travelling behind a bus that pulls up at a bus stop. What should you do?

Mark two answers
- A. Accelerate past the bus sounding your horn
- ☑ B. Watch carefully for pedestrians
- ☑ C. Be ready to give way to the bus
- D. Pull in closely behind the bus

403 When you approach a bus signalling to move off from a bus stop you should

Mark one answer
- A. get past before it moves
- ☑ B. allow it to pull away, if it is safe to do so
- C. flash your headllights as you approach
- D. signal left and wave the bus on

404 Which of these vehicles is LEAST likely to be affected by crosswinds?

Mark one answer
- A. Cyclists
- B. Motorcyclists
- C. High-sided vehicles
- ☑ D. Cars

405 You are following a large lorry on a wet road. Spray makes it difficult to see. You should

Mark one answer
- ☑ A. drop back until you can see better
- B. put your headlights on full beam
- C. keep close to the lorry, away from the spray
- D. speed up and overtake quickly

406 Some two-way roads are divided into three lanes. Why are these particularly dangerous?

Mark one answer
- ☑ A. Traffic in both directions can use the middle lane to overtake
- B. Traffic can travel faster in poor weather conditions
- C. Traffic can overtake on the left
- D. Traffic uses the middle lane for emergencies only

407

What should you do as you approach this lorry?

Mark one answer

- ☑ **A.** Slow down and be prepared to wait
- ☐ **B.** Make the lorry wait for you
- ☐ **C.** Flash your lights at the lorry
- ☐ **D.** Move to the right-hand side of the road

408

You are following a large articulated vehicle. It is going to turn left into a narrow road. What action should you take?

Mark one answer

- ☐ **A.** Move out and overtake on the right
- ☐ **B.** Pass on the left as the vehicle moves out
- ☑ **C.** Be prepared to stop behind
- ☐ **D.** Overtake quickly before the lorry moves out

409

You keep well back while waiting to overtake a large vehicle. A car fills the gap. You should

Mark one answer

- ☐ **A.** sound your horn
- ☑ **B.** drop back further
- ☐ **C.** flash your headlights
- ☐ **D.** start to overtake

410

At a junction you see this signal. It means

Mark one answer

- ☐ **A.** cars must stop
- ☑ **B.** trams must stop
- ☐ **C.** both trams and cars must stop
- ☐ **D.** both trams and cars can continue

411 It is very windy. You are behind a motorcyclist who is overtaking a high-sided vehicle. What should you do?

Mark one answer

A. Overtake the motorcyclist immediately
B. Keep well back
C. Stay level with the motorcyclist
D. Keep close to the motorcyclist

412 It is very windy. You are about to overtake a motorcyclist. You should

Mark one answer

A. overtake slowly
B. allow extra room
C. sound your horn
D. keep close as you pass

413 You are towing a caravan. Which is the safest type of rear view mirror to use?

Mark one answer

A. Interior wide-angle-view mirror
B. Extended-arm side mirrors
C. Ordinary door mirrors
D. Ordinary interior mirror

414 You are driving downhill. There is a car parked on the other side of the road. Large, slow lorries are coming towards you. You should

Mark one answer

A. keep going because you have the right of way
B. slow down and give way
C. speed up and get past quickly
D. pull over on the right behind the parked car

415 As a driver, why should you be more careful where trams operate?

Mark two answers

A. Because they do not have a horn
B. Because they do not stop for cars
C. Because they are silent
D. Because they cannot steer to avoid you
E. Because they do not have lights

416 You are driving in town. Ahead of you a bus is at a bus stop. Which TWO of the following should you do?

Mark two answers

A. Be prepared to give way if the bus suddenly moves off
B. Continue at the same speed but sound your horn as a warning
C. Watch carefully for the sudden appearance of pedestrians
D. Pass the bus as quickly as you possibly can

417 You are driving in heavy traffic on a wet road. Spray makes it difficult to be seen. You should use your

Mark two answers

- A. full beam headlights
- ☑ B. rear fog lights if visibility is less than 100 metres (328 feet)
- C. rear fog lights if visibility is more than 100 metres (328 feet)
- ☑ D. dipped headlights
- E. sidelights only

418 You are driving along this road. What should you be prepared to do?

Mark one answer

- A. Sound your horn and continue
- ☑ B. Slow down and give way
- C. Report the driver to the police
- D. Squeeze through the gap

419 You are on a wet motorway with surface spray. You should use

Mark one answer

- A. hazard flashers
- ☑ B. dipped headlights
- C. rear fog lights
- D. sidelights

420 You are following a vehicle at a safe distance on a wet road. Another driver overtakes you and pulls into the gap you have left. What should you do?

Mark one answer

- A. Flash your headlights as a warning
- B. Try to overtake safely as soon as you can
- ✓ C. Drop back to regain a safe distance
- D. Stay close to the other vehicle until it moves on

421 In which THREE of these situations may you overtake another vehicle on the left?

Mark three answers

- ✓ A. When you are in a one-way street
- B. When approaching a motorway slip road where you will be turning off
- ✓ C. When the vehicle in front is signalling to turn right
- D. When a slower vehicle is travelling in the right-hand lane of a dual carriageway
- ✓ E. In slow-moving traffic queues when traffic in the right-hand lane is moving more slowly

422 You are travelling in very heavy rain. Your overall stopping distance is likely to be

Mark one answer

- ✓ A. doubled
- B. halved
- C. up to ten times greater
- D. no different

423 Which TWO of the following are correct? When overtaking at night you should

Mark two answers

- A. wait until a bend so that you can see the oncoming headlights
- B. sound your horn twice before moving out
- ✓ C. be careful because you can see less
- ✓ D. beware of bends in the road ahead
- E. put headlights on full beam

424 You are parking on a two way road at night. The speed limit is 40mph. You should park on the

Mark one answer

- ✓ A. left with sidelights on
- B. left with no lights on
- C. right with sidelights on
- D. right with dipped headlights on

425 When may you wait in a box junction?

Mark one answer

- A. When you are stationary in a queue of traffic
- B. When approaching a pelican crossing
- C. When approaching a zebra crossing
- ✓ D. When oncoming traffic prevents you from turning right

426 Which of these plates normally appears with this road sign?

Mark one answer

☑ **A.**

Humps for ½ mile

☐ **B.**

HumpBridge

☐ **C.**

Low Bridge

☐ **D.**

Soft Verge

427 Areas reserved for trams may have

Mark three answers

☐ **A.** metal studs around them
☑ **B.** white line markings
☐ **C.** zig zag markings
☑ **D.** a different coloured surface
☐ **E.** yellow hatch markings
☑ **F.** a different surface texture

428 Traffic calming measures are used to

Mark one answer

☐ **A.** stop road rage
☐ **B.** help overtaking
☑ **C.** slow traffic down
☐ **D.** help parking

429 Why should you always reduce your speed when travelling in fog?

Mark one answer

☐ **A.** Because the brakes do not work as well
☐ **B.** Because you could be dazzled by other people's fog lights
☐ **C.** Because the engine is colder
☑ **D.** Because it is more difficult to see events ahead

430 You are on a motorway in fog. The left-hand edge of the motorway can be identified by reflective studs. What colour are they?

Mark one answer

☐ **A.** Green
☐ **B.** Amber
☑ **C.** Red
☐ **D.** White

431 A rumble device is designed to

Mark two answers

- A. give directions
- B. prevent cattle escaping
- C. alert you to low tyre pressure
- D. alert you to a hazard
- E. encourage you to reduce speed

432 You are on a narrow road at night. A slower-moving vehicle ahead has been signalling right for some time. What should you do?

Mark one answer

- A. Overtake on the left
- B. Flash your headlights before overtaking
- C. Signal right and sound your horn
- D. Wait for the signal to be cancelled before overtaking

433 Why should you test your brakes after this hazard?

Mark one answer

- A. Because you will be on a slippery road
- B. Because your brakes will be soaking wet
- C. Because you will have gone down a long hill
- D. Because you will have just crossed a long bridge

434 You have to make a journey in foggy conditions. You should

Mark one answer

- A. follow other vehicles' tail lights closely
- B. avoid using dipped headlights
- C. leave plenty of time for your journey
- D. keep two seconds behind other vehicles

435 You are overtaking a car at night. You must be sure that

Mark one answer

- A. you flash your headlights before overtaking
- B. you select a higher gear
- C. you have switched your lights to full beam before overtaking
- D. you do not dazzle other road users

436 You see a vehicle coming towards you on a single track road. You should

Mark one answer

- [ ] **A.** go back to the main road
- [ ] **B.** do an emergency stop
- [x] **C.** stop at a passing place
- [ ] **D.** put on your hazard warning lights

437 You are on a road which has speed humps. A driver in front is travelling slower than you. You should

Mark one answer

- [ ] **A.** sound your horn
- [ ] **B.** overtake as soon as you can
- [ ] **C.** flash your headlights
- [x] **D.** slow down and stay behind

438 You are following other vehicles in fog with your lights on. How else can you reduce the chances of being involved in an accident?

Mark one answer

- [ ] **A.** Keep close to the vehicle in front
- [ ] **B.** Use your main beam instead of dipped headlights
- [ ] **C.** Keep together with the faster vehicles
- [x] **D.** Reduce your speed and increase the gap

439 What are TWO main reasons why coasting downhill is wrong?

Mark two answers

- [ ] **A.** Fuel consumption will be higher
- [x] **B.** The vehicle will pick up speed
- [ ] **C.** It puts more wear and tear on the tyres
- [x] **D.** You have less braking and steering control
- [ ] **E.** It damages the engine

440 Hills can affect the performance of your vehicle. Which TWO apply when driving up steep hills?

Mark two answers

- [ ] **A.** Higher gears will pull better
- [x] **B.** You will slow down sooner
- [ ] **C.** Overtaking will be easier
- [x] **D.** The engine will work harder
- [ ] **E.** The steering will feel heavier

441 Why is coasting wrong?

Mark one answer

- [ ] **A.** It will cause the car to skid
- [ ] **B.** It will make the engine stall
- [ ] **C.** The engine will run faster
- [x] **D.** There is no engine braking

442 You are driving on the motorway in windy conditions. When passing high-sided vehicles you should

Mark one answer

- [ ] **A.** increase your speed
- [x] **B.** be wary of a sudden gust
- [ ] **C.** drive alongside very closely
- [ ] **D.** expect normal conditions

443 To correct a rear-wheel skid you should

Mark one answer

- [ ] **A.** not steer at all
- [ ] **B.** steer away from it
- [x] **C.** steer into it
- [ ] **D.** apply your handbrake

444 You are driving in very wet weather. Your vehicle begins to slide. This effect is called

Mark one answer

- [ ] **A.** hosing
- [ ] **B.** weaving
- [x] **C.** aquaplaning
- [ ] **D.** fading

445 You have to make a journey in fog. What are the TWO most important things you should do before you set out?

Mark two answers

- [ ] **A.** Top up the radiator with antifreeze
- [ ] **B.** Make sure that you have a warning triangle in the vehicle
- [x] **C.** Check that your lights are working
- [ ] **D.** Check the battery
- [x] **E.** Make sure that the windows are clean

446 You are driving in fog. Why should you keep well back from the vehicle in front?

Mark one answer

- [ ] **A.** In case it changes direction suddenly
- [ ] **B.** In case its fog lights dazzle you
- [x] **C.** In case it stops suddenly
- [ ] **D.** In case its brake lights dazzle you

447 You should switch your rear fog lights on when visibility drops below

Mark one answer

- [ ] **A.** your overall stopping distance
- [ ] **B.** ten car lengths
- [ ] **C.** 200 metres (656 feet)
- [x] **D.** 100 metres (328 feet)

448 Whilst driving, the fog clears and you can see more clearly. You must remember to

Mark one answer

- [x] **A.** switch off the fog lights
- [ ] **B.** reduce your speed
- [ ] **C.** switch off the demister
- [ ] **D.** close any open windows

449 You have to park on the road in fog. You should

Mark one answer

- [x] **A.** leave sidelights on
- [ ] **B.** leave dipped headlights and fog lights on
- [ ] **C.** leave dipped headlights on
- [ ] **D.** leave main beam headlights on

450 On a foggy day you unavoidably have to park your car on the road. You should

Mark one answer

- [ ] **A.** leave your headlights on
- [ ] **B.** leave your fog lights on
- [✓] **C.** leave your sidelights on
- [ ] **D.** leave your hazard lights on

451 You are travelling at night. You are dazzled by headlights coming towards you. You should

Mark one answer

- [ ] **A.** pull down your sun visor
- [✓] **B.** slow down or stop
- [ ] **C.** switch on your main beam headlights
- [ ] **D.** put your hand over your eyes

452 Which of the following may apply when dealing with this hazard?

Mark four answers

- [✓] **A.** It could be more difficult in winter
- [✓] **B.** Use a low gear and drive slowly
- [ ] **C.** Use a high gear to prevent wheelspin
- [✓] **D.** Test your brakes afterwards
- [ ] **E.** Always switch on fog lamps
- [✓] **F.** There may be a depth gauge

453 Front fog lights may be used ONLY if

Mark one answer

- [✓] **A.** visibility is seriously reduced
- [ ] **B.** they are fitted above the bumper
- [ ] **C.** they are not as bright as the headlights
- [ ] **D.** an audible warning device is used

454 Front fog lights may be used ONLY if

Mark one answer

- [ ] **A.** your headlights are not working
- [ ] **B.** they are operated with rear fog lights
- [ ] **C.** they were fitted by the vehicle manufacturer
- [✓] **D.** visibility is seriously reduced

455 You are driving with your front fog lights switched on. Earlier fog has now cleared. What should you do?

Mark one answer

- [ ] **A.** Leave them on if other drivers have their lights on
- [✓] **B.** Switch them off as long as visibility remains good
- [ ] **C.** Flash them to warn oncoming traffic that is foggy
- [ ] **D.** Drive with them on instead of your headlights

156 Front fog lights should be used ONLY when

Mark one answer

A. travelling in very light rain
☑ B. visibility is seriously reduced
C. daylight is fading
D. driving after midnight

157 Why is it dangerous to leave rear fog lights on when they are not needed?

Mark two answers

☑ A. Brake lights are less clear
☑ B. Following drivers can be dazzled
C. Electrical systems could be overloaded
D. Direction indicators may not work properly
E. The battery could fail

158 You are driving on a clear dry night with your rear fog lights switched on. This may

Mark two answers

A. reduce glare from the road surface
☑ B. make other drivers think you are braking
C. give a better view of the road ahead
☑ D. dazzle following drivers
E. help your indicators to be seen more clearly

459 While you are driving in fog, it becomes necessary to use front fog lights. You should

Mark one answer

A. only turn them on in heavy traffic conditions
B. remember not to use them on motorways
C. only use them with dipped headlights
☑ D. remember to switch them off as visibility improves

460 You have just driven out of fog. Visibility is now good. You MUST

Mark one answer

☑ A. switch off all your fog lights
B. keep your rear fog lights on
C. keep your front fog lights on
D. leave fog lights on in case fog returns

461 You forget to switch off your rear fog lights when the fog has cleared. This may

Mark three answers

☑ A. dazzle other road users
B. reduce battery life
☑ C. cause brake lights to be less clear
☑ D. be breaking the law
E. seriously affect engine power

462 You have been driving in thick fog which has now cleared. You must switch OFF your rear fog lights because

Mark one answer

- [ ] **A.** they use a lot of power from the battery
- [✓] **B.** they make your brake lights less clear
- [ ] **C.** they will cause dazzle in your rear view mirrors
- [ ] **D.** they may not be properly adjusted

463 Front fog lights should be used

Mark one answer

- [✓] **A.** when visibility is reduced to 100 metres (328 feet)
- [ ] **B.** as a warning to oncoming traffic
- [ ] **C.** when driving during the hours of darkness
- [ ] **D.** in any conditions and at any time

464 Using rear fog lights in clear daylight will

Mark one answer

- [ ] **A.** be useful when towing a trailer
- [ ] **B.** give extra protection
- [✓] **C.** dazzle other drivers
- [ ] **D.** make following drivers keep back

465 Using front fog lights in clear daylight will

Mark one answer

- [ ] **A.** flatten the battery
- [✓] **B.** dazzle other drivers
- [ ] **C.** improve your visibility
- [ ] **D.** increase your awareness

466 You may use front fog lights with headlights ONLY when visibility is reduced to less than

Mark one answer

- [✓] **A.** 100 metres (328 feet)
- [ ] **B.** 200 metres (656 feet)
- [ ] **C.** 300 metres (984 feet)
- [ ] **D.** 400 metres (1312 feet)

467 You may drive with front fog lights switched on

N 512 CTW

Mark one answer

- [✓] **A.** when visibility is less than 100 metres (328 feet)
- [ ] **B.** at any time to be noticed
- [ ] **C.** instead of headlights on high speed road
- [ ] **D.** when dazzled by the lights of oncoming vehicles

468 Chains can be fitted to your wheels to help prevent

Mark one answer

- [ ] **A.** damage to the road surface
- [ ] **B.** wear to the tyres
- [✓] **C.** skidding in deep snow
- [ ] **D.** the brakes locking

469
You are driving down a long steep hill. You suddenly notice your brakes are not working as well as normal. What is the usual cause of this?

Mark one answer

☑ **A.** The brakes overheating
☐ **B.** Air in the brake fluid
☐ **C.** Oil on the brakes
☐ **D.** Badly adjusted brakes

470
Pressing the clutch pedal down or rolling in neutral for too long while driving will

Mark one answer

☐ **A.** use more fuel
☐ **B.** cause the engine to overheat
☑ **C.** reduce your control
☐ **D.** improve tyre wear

471
How can you use the engine of your vehicle to control your speed?

Mark one answer

☑ **A.** By changing to a lower gear
☐ **B.** By selecting reverse gear
☐ **C.** By changing to a higher gear
☐ **D.** By selecting neutral

472
You are driving down a steep hill. Why could keeping the clutch down or selecting neutral for too long be dangerous?

Mark one answer

☐ **A.** Fuel consumption will be higher
☑ **B.** Your vehicle will pick up speed
☐ **C.** It will damage the engine
☐ **D.** It will wear tyres out more quickly

473
Why could keeping the clutch down or selecting neutral for long periods of time be dangerous?

Mark one answer

☐ **A.** Fuel spillage will occur
☐ **B.** Engine damage may be caused
☑ **C.** You will have less steering and braking control
☐ **D.** It will wear tyres out more quickly

474
You are driving on an icy road. What distance should you drive from the car in front?

Mark one answer

☐ **A.** Four times the normal distance
☐ **B.** Six times the normal distance
☐ **C.** Eight times the normal distance
☑ **D.** Ten times the normal distance

475
You are on a well-lit motorway at night. You must

Mark one answer

☐ **A.** use only your sidelights
☑ **B.** always use your headlights
☐ **C.** always use rear fog lights
☐ **D.** use headlights only in bad weather

476 You are on a motorway at night with other vehicles just ahead of you. Which lights should you have on?

Mark one answer

- A. Front fog lights
- B. Main beam headlights
- C. Sidelights only
- ☑ D. Dipped headlights

477 Which THREE of the following will affect your stopping distance?

Mark three answers

- ☑ A. How fast you are going
- ☑ B. The tyres on your vehicle
- C. The time of day
- ☑ D. The weather
- E. The street lighting

478 You are on a motorway at night. You MUST have your headlights switched on unless

Mark one answer

- A. there are vehicles close in front of you
- B. you are travelling below 50mph
- C. the motorway is lit
- ☑ D. your vehicle is broken down on the hard shoulder

479 When snow is falling heavily you should

Mark one answer

- A. drive provided you use your headlights
- B. not drive unless you have a mobile phone
- C. drive only when your journey is short
- ☑ D. not drive unless it is essential

480 Which FOUR of these must NOT use motorways?

Mark four answers

- [✓] **A.** Learner car drivers
- [ ] **B.** Motorcycles over 50cc
- [ ] **C.** Double-decker buses
- [✓] **D.** Farm tractors
- [✓] **E.** Horse riders
- [✓] **F.** Cyclists

481 Which FOUR of these must NOT use motorways?

Mark four answers

- [✓] **A.** Learner car drivers
- [ ] **B.** Motorcycles over 50cc
- [ ] **C.** Double-decker buses
- [✓] **D.** Farm tractors
- [✓] **E.** Learner motorcyclists
- [✓] **F.** Cyclists

482 Immediately after joining a motorway you should normally

Mark one answer

- [ ] **A.** try to overtake
- [ ] **B.** readjust your mirrors
- [ ] **C.** position your vehicle in the centre lane
- [✓] **D.** keep in the left lane

483 When joining a motorway you must always

Mark one answer

- [ ] **A.** use the hard shoulder
- [ ] **B.** stop at the end of the acceleration lane
- [ ] **C.** come to a stop before joining the motorway
- [✓] **D.** give way to traffic already on the motorway

484 What is the national speed limit for cars and motorcycles in the centre lane of a three-lane motorway?

Mark one answer

- [ ] **A.** 40mph
- [ ] **B.** 50mph
- [ ] **C.** 60mph
- [✓] **D.** 70mph

485 What is the national speed limit on motorways for cars and motorcycles?

Mark one answer

- [ ] **A.** 30mph
- [ ] **B.** 50mph
- [ ] **C.** 60mph
- [✓] **D.** 70mph

486 The left-hand lane on a three-lane motorway is for use by

Mark one answer

- [x] **A.** any vehicle
- [ ] **B.** large vehicles only
- [ ] **C.** emergency vehicles only
- [ ] **D.** slow vehicles only

487 What is the right-hand lane used for on a three-lane motorway?

Mark one answer

- [ ] **A.** Emergency vehicles only
- [x] **B.** Overtaking
- [ ] **C.** Vehicles towing trailers
- [ ] **D.** Coaches only

488 Which of these IS NOT allowed to travel in the right-hand lane of a three-lane motorway?

Mark one answer

- [ ] **A.** A small delivery van
- [ ] **B.** A motorcycle
- [x] **C.** A vehicle towing a trailer
- [ ] **D.** A motorcycle and side-car

489 On motorways you should never overtake on the left UNLESS

Mark one answer

- [ ] **A.** you can see well ahead that the hard shoulder is clear
- [ ] **B.** the traffic in the right-hand lane is signalling right
- [ ] **C.** you warn drivers behind by signalling left
- [x] **D.** there is a queue of traffic to your right th is moving more slowly

490 You are travelling on a motorway. You decide you need a rest. You should

Mark two answers

- [ ] **A.** stop on the hard shoulder
- [x] **B.** go to a service area
- [ ] **C.** park on the slip road
- [ ] **D.** park on the central reservation
- [x] **E.** leave at the next exit

491 You break down on a motorway. Yo need to call for help. Why may it be better to use an emergency roadsid telephone rather than a mobile phone?

Mark one answer

- [ ] **A.** It connects you to a local garage
- [ ] **B.** Using a mobile phone will distract other drivers
- [x] **C.** It allows easy location by the emergency services
- [ ] **D.** Mobile phones do not work on motorway

492
What should you use the hard shoulder of a motorway for?

Mark one answer
- ☑ **A.** Stopping in an emergency
- ☐ **B.** Leaving the motorway
- ☐ **C.** Stopping when you are tired
- ☐ **D.** Joining the motorway

493
After a breakdown you need to rejoin the main carriageway of a motorway from the hard shoulder. You should

Mark one answer
- ☐ **A.** move out onto the carriageway then build up your speed
- ☐ **B.** move out onto the carriageway using your hazard lights
- ☑ **C.** gain speed on the hard shoulder before moving out onto the carriageway
- ☐ **D.** wait on the hard shoulder until someone flashes their headlights at you

494
A crawler lane on a motorway is found

Mark one answer
- ☑ **A.** on a steep gradient
- ☐ **B.** before a service area
- ☐ **C.** before a junction
- ☐ **D.** along the hard shoulder

495
You are on a motorway. There are red flashing lights above every lane. You must

Mark one answer
- ☐ **A.** pull onto the hard shoulder
- ☐ **B.** slow down and watch for further signals
- ☐ **C.** leave at the next exit
- ☑ **D.** stop and wait

496
You are in the right-hand lane on a motorway. You see these overhead signs. This means

Mark one answer

- ☑ **A.** move to the left and reduce your speed to 50mph
- ☐ **B.** there are roadworks 50 metres (55 yards) ahead
- ☐ **C.** use the hard shoulder until you have passed the hazard
- ☐ **D.** leave the motorway at the next exit

497
What do these motorway signs show?

Mark one answer

- ☐ **A.** They are countdown markers to a bridge
- ☐ **B.** They are distance markers to the next telephone
- ☑ **C.** They are countdown markers to the next exit
- ☐ **D.** They warn of a police control ahead

498
On a motorway the amber reflective studs can be found between

Mark one answer

- ☐ **A.** the hard shoulder and the carriageway
- ☐ **B.** the acceleration lane and the carriageway
- ☑ **C.** the central reservation and the carriageway
- ☐ **D.** each pair of the lanes

499
What colour are the reflective studs between the lanes on a motorway?

Mark one answer

- ☐ **A.** Green
- ☐ **B.** Amber
- ☑ **C.** White
- ☐ **D.** Red

500
What colour are the reflective studs between a motorway and its slip road?

Mark one answer

- ☐ **A.** Amber
- ☐ **B.** White
- ☑ **C.** Green
- ☐ **D.** Red

501
You are allowed to stop on a motorway when you

Mark one answer

- ☐ **A.** need to walk and get fresh air
- ☐ **B.** wish to pick up hitch hikers
- ☑ **C.** are told to do so by flashing red lights
- ☐ **D.** need to use a mobile telephone

502 You have broken down on a motorway. To find the nearest emergency telephone you should always walk

Mark one answer

- [ ] A. with the traffic flow
- [ ] B. facing oncoming traffic
- [x] C. in the direction shown on the marker posts
- [ ] D. in the direction of the nearest exit

503 You are travelling along the left lane of a three-lane motorway. Traffic is joining from a slip road. You should

Mark one answer

- [ ] A. race the other vehicles
- [x] B. move to another lane
- [ ] C. maintain a steady speed
- [ ] D. switch on your hazard flashers

504 You are approaching road works on a motorway. You should

Mark one answer

- [ ] A. speed up to clear the works quickly
- [ ] B. always use the hard shoulder
- [x] C. obey all speed limits
- [ ] D. stay very close to the vehicle in front

505 You are joining a motorway. Why is it important to make full use of the slip road?

Mark one answer

- [ ] A. Because there is space available to turn round if you need to
- [ ] B. To allow you direct access to the overtaking lanes
- [x] C. To build up a speed similar to traffic on the motorway
- [ ] D. Because you can continue on the hard shoulder

506 How should you use the emergency telephone on a motorway?

Mark one answer

- [ ] A. Stay close to the carriageway
- [x] B. Face the oncoming traffic
- [ ] C. Keep your back to the traffic
- [ ] D. Stand on the hard shoulder

507 You are on a motorway. What colour are the reflective studs on the left of the carriageway?

Mark one answer

- [ ] A. Green
- [x] B. Red
- [ ] C. White
- [ ] D. Amber

508 On a three-lane motorway which lane should you normally use?

Mark one answer

- [x] A. Left
- [ ] B. Right
- [ ] C. Centre
- [ ] D. Either the right or centre

509 A basic rule when on motorways is

Mark one answer
- [ ] A. use the lane that has least traffic
- [x] B. keep to the left lane unless overtaking
- [ ] C. overtake on the side that is clearest
- [ ] D. try to keep above 50mph to prevent congestion

510 When going through a contraflow system on a motorway you should

Mark one answer
- [ ] A. ensure that you do not exceed 30mph
- [x] B. keep a good distance from the vehicle ahead
- [ ] C. switch lanes to keep the traffic flowing
- [ ] D. stay close to the vehicle ahead to reduce queues

511 You are on a three-lane motorway. There are red reflective studs on your left and white ones to your right. Where are you?

Mark one answer
- [ ] A. In the right-hand lane
- [ ] B. In the middle lane
- [ ] C. On the hard shoulder
- [x] D. In the left-hand lane

512 When may you stop on a motorway?

Mark three answers
- [ ] A. If you have to read a map
- [ ] B. When you are tired and need a rest
- [x] C. If red lights show above every lane
- [x] D. When told to by the police
- [ ] E. If your mobile phone rings
- [x] F. In an emergency or a breakdown

513 As a provisional licence-holder you should not drive a car

Mark one answer
- [ ] A. over 50mph
- [ ] B. at night
- [x] C. on the motorway
- [ ] D. with passengers in rear seats

514 You are towing a trailer on a motorway. What is your maximum speed limit?

Mark one answer
- A. 40mph
- B. 50mph
- C. 60mph
- D. 70mph

515 The left-hand lane of a motorway should be used for

Mark one answer
- A. breakdowns and emergencies only
- B. overtaking slower traffic in the other lanes
- C. slow vehicles only
- D. normal driving

516 You are driving on a motorway. You have to slow down quickly due to a hazard. You should

Mark one answer
- A. switch on your hazard lights
- B. switch on your headlights
- C. sound your horn
- D. flash your headlights

517 You get a puncture on the motorway. You manage to get your vehicle on to the hard shoulder. You should

Mark one answer
- A. change the wheel yourself immediately
- ☑ B. use the emergency telephone and call for assistance
- C. try to wave down another vehicle for help
- D. only change the wheel if you have a passenger to help you

518 You are driving on a motorway. By mistake, you go past the exit that you wanted to take. You should

Mark one answer
- A. carefully reverse on the hard shoulder
- ☑ B. carry on to the next exit
- C. carefully reverse in the left-hand lane
- D. make a U-turn at the next gap in the central reservation

519 Your vehicle breaks down on the hard shoulder of a motorway. You decide to use your mobile phone to call for help. You should

Mark one answer
- A. stand at the rear of the vehicle while making the call
- B. try to repair the vehicle yourself
- C. get out of the vehicle by the right-hand door
- ☑ D. check your location from the marker posts on the left

520 You are driving a car on a motorway. Unless signs show otherwise you must NOT exceed

Mark one answer
- [ ] **A.** 50mph
- [ ] **B.** 60mph
- [x] **C.** 70mph
- [ ] **D.** 80mph

521 You are on a three-lane motorway towing a trailer. You may use the right hand lane when

Mark one answer
- [x] **A.** there are lane closures
- [ ] **B.** there is slow moving traffic
- [ ] **C.** you can maintain a high speed
- [ ] **D.** large vehicles are in the left and centre lanes

522 You are on a motorway. There is a contraflow system ahead. What would you expect to find?

Mark one answer
- [x] **A.** Temporary traffic lights
- [ ] **B.** Lower speed limits
- [ ] **C.** Wider lanes than normal
- [ ] **D.** Speed humps

523 You are driving at 70mph on a three-lane motorway. There is no traffic ahead. Which lane should you use?

Mark one answer
- [ ] **A.** Any lane
- [ ] **B.** Middle lane
- [ ] **C.** Right lane
- [x] **D.** Left lane

524 Your vehicle has broken down on a motorway. You are not able to stop on the hard shoulder. What should you do ?

Mark one answer
- [x] **A.** Switch on your hazard warning lights
- [ ] **B.** Stop following traffic and ask for help
- [ ] **C.** Attempt to repair your vehicle quickly
- [ ] **D.** Stand behind your vehicle to warn other

525 Why is it particularly important to carry out a check on your vehicle before making a long motorway journey?

Mark one answer
- [ ] **A.** You will have to do more harsh braking motorways
- [ ] **B.** Motorway service stations do not deal with breakdowns
- [ ] **C.** The road surface will wear down the tyres faster
- [x] **D.** Continuous high speeds may increase the risk of your vehicle breaking down

526 For what reason may you use the right-hand lane of a motorway?

ark one answer

- **A.** For keeping out of the way of lorries
- **B.** For driving at more than 70mph
- **C.** For turning right
- ☑ **D.** For overtaking other vehicles

527 On a motorway you may ONLY stop on the hard shoulder

ark one answer

- ☑ **A.** in an emergency
- **B.** if you feel tired and need to rest
- **C.** if you accidentally go past the exit that you wanted to take
- **D.** to pick up a hitchhiker

528 You are driving on a motorway. The car ahead shows its hazard lights for a short time. This tells you that

Mark one answer

- **A.** the driver wants you to overtake
- **B.** the other car is going to change lanes
- ☑ **C.** traffic ahead is slowing or stopping suddenly
- **D.** there is a police speed check ahead

529 The emergency telephones on a motorway are connected to the

Mark one answer

- **A.** ambulance service
- ☑ **B.** police control
- **C.** fire brigade
- **D.** breakdown service

530 You are intending to leave the motorway at the next exit. Before you reach the exit you should normally position your vehicle

Mark one answer

- **A.** in the middle lane
- ☑ **B.** in the left-hand lane
- **C.** on the hard shoulder
- **D.** in any lane

531 What is the meaning of this sign?

Mark one answer

- A. Local speed limit applies
- B. No waiting on the carriageway
- C. National speed limit applies
- D. No entry to vehicular traffic

532 What is the national speed limit on a single carriageway road for cars and motorcycles?

Mark one answer

- A. 70mph
- B. 60mph
- C. 50mph
- D. 30mph

533 What is the national speed limit for cars and motorcycles on a dual carriageway?

Mark one answer

- A. 30mph
- B. 50mph
- C. 60mph
- D. 70mph

534 There are no speed limit signs on the road. How is a 30mph limit indicated?

Mark one answer

- A. By hazard warning lines
- B. By street lighting
- C. By pedestrian islands
- D. By double or single yellow lines

535 Where you see street lights but no speed limit signs the limit is usually

Mark one answer

- A. 30mph
- B. 40mph
- C. 50mph
- D. 60mph

536 What does this sign mean?

Mark one answer

- A. Minimum speed 30mph
- B. End of maximum speed
- C. End of minimum speed
- D. Maximum speed 30mph

537
There is a tractor ahead of you. You wish to overtake but you are NOT sure if it is safe to do so. You should

Mark one answer

- A. follow another overtaking vehicle through
- B. sound your horn to the slow vehicle to pull over
- C. speed through but flash your lights to oncoming traffic
- D. not overtake if you are in doubt

538
Which three of the following are most likely to take an unusual course at roundabouts?

Mark three answers

- A. Horse riders
- B. Milk floats
- C. Delivery vans
- D. Long vehicles
- E. Estate cars
- F. Cyclists

539
In which FOUR places must you NOT park or wait?

Mark four answers

- A. On a dual carriageway
- B. At a bus stop
- C. On the slope of a hill
- D. Opposite a traffic island
- E. In front of someone else's drive
- F. On the brow of a hill

540
In which TWO places must you NOT park?

Mark two answers

- ☑ A. Near a school entrance
- ☐ B. Near a police station
- ☐ C. In a side road
- ☑ D. At a bus stop
- ☐ E. In a one-way street

541
On a clearway you must not stop

Mark one answer

- ☑ A. at any time
- ☐ B. when it is busy
- ☐ C. in the rush hour
- ☐ D. during daylight hours

542
What is the meaning of this sign?

Mark one answer

- ☐ A. No entry
- ☑ B. Waiting restrictions
- ☐ C. National speed limit
- ☐ D. School crossing patrol

543
You park overnight on a road with a 40mph speed limit. You should

Mark one answer

- ☐ A. park facing the traffic
- ☑ B. park with sidelights on
- ☐ C. park with dipped headlights on
- ☐ D. park near a street light

544 You can park on the right-hand side of a road at night

Mark one answer
- [x] **A.** in a one-way street
- [ ] **B.** with your sidelights on
- [ ] **C.** more than 10 metres (32 feet) from a junction
- [ ] **D.** under a lamp-post

545 On a three-lane dual carriageway the right-hand lane can be used for

Mark one answer
- [ ] **A.** overtaking only, never turning right
- [x] **B.** overtaking or turning right
- [ ] **C.** fast-moving traffic only
- [ ] **D.** turning right only, never overtaking

546 You are entering an area of roadworks. There is a temporary speed limit displayed. You must

Mark one answer
- [x] **A.** not exceed the speed limit
- [ ] **B.** obey the limit only during rush hour
- [ ] **C.** accept the speed limit as advisable
- [ ] **D.** obey the limit except for overnight

547 You are approaching a busy juncti There are several lanes with road markings. At the last moment you realise that you are in the wrong lane. You should

Mark one answer
- [ ] **A.** continue in that lane
- [ ] **B.** force your way across
- [ ] **C.** stop until the area has cleared
- [ ] **D.** use clear arm signals to cut across

548 Where may you overtake on a one-way street?

Mark one answer
- [ ] **A.** Only on the left-hand side
- [ ] **B.** Overtaking is not allowed
- [ ] **C.** Only on the right-hand side
- [x] **D.** Either on the right or the left

549 Signals are normally given by direction indicators and

Mark one answer
- [x] **A.** brake lights
- [ ] **B.** sidelights
- [ ] **C.** fog lights
- [ ] **D.** interior lights

550 When going straight ahead at a roundabout you should

Mark one answer
- [x] **A.** indicate left before leaving the roundab
- [ ] **B.** not indicate at any time
- [ ] **C.** indicate right when approaching the roundabout
- [ ] **D.** indicate left when approaching the roundabout

51 Which vehicle might have to use a different course to normal at roundabouts?

rk one answer

A. Sports car   B. Van
C. Estate car   ☑ D. Long vehicle

52 You are going straight ahead at a roundabout. How should you signal?

rk one answer

A. Signal right on the approach and then left to leave the roundabout
B. Signal left as you leave the roundabout
C. Signal left on the approach to the roundabout and keep the signal on until you leave
D. Signal left just after you pass the exit before the one you will take

53 At a crossroads there are no signs or road markings. Two vehicles approach. Which has priority?

rk one answer

A. Neither vehicle
B. The vehicle travelling the fastest
C. The vehicle on the widest road
D. Vehicles approaching from the right

54 The dual carriageway you are turning right on to has a narrow central reserve. You should

rk one answer

A. proceed to the central reserve and wait
B. wait until the road is clear in both directions
C. stop in the first lane so that other vehicles give way
D. emerge slightly to show your intentions

555 You may only enter a box junction when

Mark one answer

A. there are less than two vehicles in front of you
B. the traffic lights show green
☑ C. your exit road is clear
D. you need to turn left

556 You may wait in a yellow box junction when

Mark one answer

☑ A. oncoming traffic is preventing you from turning right
B. you are in a queue of traffic turning left
C. you are in a queue of traffic to go ahead
D. you are on a roundabout

557 You MUST stop when signalled to do so by which THREE of these?

Mark three answers

- ☑ **A.** A police officer
- ☐ **B.** A pedestrian
- ☑ **C.** A school crossing patrol
- ☐ **D.** A bus driver
- ☑ **E.** A red traffic light

558 At roadworks which of the following can control traffic flow?

Mark three answers

- ☑ **A.** A STOP–GO board
- ☐ **B.** Flashing amber lights
- ☑ **C.** A policeman
- ☐ **D.** Flashing red lights
- ☑ **E.** Temporary traffic lights

559 You will see these markers when approaching

Mark one answer

- ☐ **A.** the end of a motorway
- ☑ **B.** a concealed level crossing
- ☐ **C.** a concealed speed limit sign
- ☐ **D.** the end of a dual carriageway

560 Someone is waiting to cross at a zebra crossing. They are standing the pavement. You should normal

Mark one answer

- ☐ **A.** go on quickly before they step onto the crossing
- ☐ **B.** stop before you reach the zig zag lines let them cross
- ☑ **C.** stop, let them cross, wait patiently
- ☐ **D.** ignore them as they are still on the pavem

561 At toucan crossings, apart from pedestrians you should be aware

Mark one answer

- ☐ **A.** emergency vehicles emerging
- ☐ **B.** buses pulling out
- ☐ **C.** trams crossing in front
- ☑ **D.** cyclists riding across

562 Who can use a toucan crossing?

Mark two answers

- ☐ **A.** Trains
- ☑ **B.** Cyclists
- ☐ **C.** Buses
- ☑ **D.** Pedestrians
- ☐ **E.** Trams

563 At a pelican crossing, what does a flashing amber light mean?

Mark one answer

- A. You must not move off until the lights stop flashing
- B. You must give way to pedestrians still on the crossing
- C. You can move off, even if pedestrians are still on the crossing
- D. You must stop because the lights are about to change to red

564 You are waiting at a pelican crossing. The red light changes to flashing amber. This means you must

Mark one answer

- A. wait for pedestrians on the crossing to clear
- B. move off immediately without any hesitation
- C. wait for the green light before moving off
- D. get ready and go when the continuous amber light shows

565 You are travelling on a well-lit road at night in a built-up area. By using dipped headlights you will be able to

Mark one answer

- A. see further along the road
- B. go at a much faster speed
- C. switch to main beam quickly
- D. be easily seen by others

566 When can you park on the left opposite these road markings?

Mark one answer

- A. If the line nearest to you is broken
- B. When there are no yellow lines
- ☑ C. To pick up or set down passengers
- D. During daylight hours only

567 You are intending to turn right at a crossroads. An oncoming driver is also turning right. It will normally be safer to

Mark one answer

- ☑ A. keep the other vehicle to your RIGHT and turn behind it (offside to offside)
- B. keep the other vehicle to your LEFT and turn in front of it (nearside to nearside)
- C. carry on and turn at the next junction instead
- D. hold back and wait for the other driver to turn first

568 You are on a road that has no traffic signs. There are street lights. What is the speed limit?

Mark one answer

- A. 20mph
- ☑ B. 30mph
- C. 40mph
- D. 60mph

569 You are going along a street with parked vehicles on the left-hand side. For which THREE reasons should you keep your speed down?

Mark three answers

- A. So that oncoming traffic can see you more clearly
- B. You may set off car alarms
- ☑ C. Vehicles may be pulling out
- ☑ D. Drivers' doors may open
- ☑ E. Children may run out from between the vehicles

570 You meet an obstruction on your side of the road. You should

Mark one answer

- A. carry on, you have priority
- ☑ B. give way to oncoming traffic
- C. wave oncoming vehicles through
- D. accelerate to get past first

571 You are on a two-lane dual carriageway. For which TWO of the following would you use the right-hand lane?

Mark two answers

- ☑ A. Turning right
- B. Normal progress
- C. Staying at the minimum allowed speed
- D. Constant high speed
- ☑ E. Overtaking slower traffic
- F. Mending punctures

572 Who has priority at an unmarked crossroads?

Mark one answer

- A. The larger vehicle
- ☑ B. No one has priority
- C. The faster vehicle
- D. The smaller vehicle

573 What is the nearest you may park a junction?

Mark one answer

- ☑ A. 10 metres (32 feet)
- B. 12 metres (39 feet)
- C. 15 metres (49 feet)
- D. 20 metres (66 feet)

574 In which THREE places must you NOT park?

Mark three answers

- ☑ A. Near the brow of a hill
- ☑ B. At or near a bus stop
- C. Where there is no pavement
- ☑ D. Within 10 metres (32 feet) of a junction
- E. On a 40mph road

575 You are waiting at a level crossing. A train has passed but the lights keep flashing. You must

ark one answer
- A. carry on waiting
- B. phone the signal operator
- C. edge over the stop line and look for trains
- D. park and investigate

576 You may drive over a footpath

ark one answer
- A. to overtake slow-moving traffic
- B. when the pavement is very wide
- C. if no pedestrians are near
- D. to get into a property

577 A single carriageway road has this sign. What is the maximum permitted speed for a car towing a trailer?

ark one answer
- A. 30mph
- B. 40mph
- C. 50mph
- D. 60mph

578 You are towing a small caravan on a dual carriageway. You must not exceed

Mark one answer
- A. 50mph
- B. 40mph
- C. 70mph
- D. 60mph ✓

579 You are finding it difficult to find a parking place in a busy town. You can see there is space on the zig zag lines of a zebra crossing. Can you park there?

Mark one answer
- A. No, unless you stay with your car
- B. Yes, in order to drop off a passenger
- C. Yes, if you do not block people from crossing
- D. No, not in any circumstances ✓

580 You want to park and you see this sign. On the days and times shown you should

Mark one answer
- [ ] **A.** park in a bay and not pay
- [ ] **B.** park on yellow lines and pay
- [ ] **C.** park on yellow lines and not pay
- [x] **D.** park in a bay and pay

581 While driving, you approach roadworks. You see a temporary maximum speed limit sign. You must

Mark one answer
- [ ] **A.** comply with the sign during the working day
- [x] **B.** comply with the sign at all times
- [ ] **C.** comply with the sign when the lanes are narrow
- [ ] **D.** comply with the sign during the hours of darkness

582 You may drive a motor car in this bus lane

Mark one answer
- [x] **A.** outside its operation hours
- [ ] **B.** to get to the front of a traffic queue
- [ ] **C.** at no times at all
- [ ] **D.** to overtake slow moving traffic

583 As a car driver which THREE lanes ⟨ you NOT normally allowed to use?

Mark three answers
- [ ] **A.** Crawler lane
- [x] **B.** Bus lane
- [ ] **C.** Overtaking lane
- [ ] **D.** Acceleration lane
- [x] **E.** Cycle lane
- [x] **F.** Tram lane

584 You are driving along a road that h⟩ a cycle lane. The lane is marked by solid white line. This means that during its period of operation

Mark one answer
- [ ] **A.** the lane may be used for parking your ca⟩
- [ ] **B.** you may drive in that lane at any time
- [ ] **C.** the lane may be used when necessary
- [x] **D.** you must not drive in that lane

585 A cycle lane is marked by a solid white line. You must not drive or park in it

Mark one answer
- [ ] **A.** at any time
- [ ] **B.** during the rush hour
- [ ] **C.** if a cyclist is using it
- [ ] **D.** during its period of operation

586 While driving, you intend to turn left into a minor road. On the approach you should

Mark one answer
- [ ] **A.** keep just left of the middle of the road
- [ ] **B.** keep in the middle of the road
- [ ] **C.** swing out wide just before turning
- [ ] **D.** keep well to the left of the road

587 You are waiting at a level crossing. The red warning lights continue to flash after a train has passed by. What should you do?

Mark one answer
- [ ] **A.** Get out and investigate
- [ ] **B.** Telephone the signal operator
- [ ] **C.** Continue to wait
- [ ] **D.** Drive across carefully

588 You are driving over a level crossing. The warning lights come on and a bell rings. What should you do?

Mark one answer
- [ ] **A.** Get everyone out of the vehicle immediately
- [ ] **B.** Stop and reverse back to clear the crossing
- [x] **C.** Keep going and clear the crossing
- [ ] **D.** Stop immediately and use your hazard warning lights

589 You are on a busy main road and find that you are travelling in the wrong direction. What should you do?

Mark one answer
- [ ] **A.** Turn into a side road on the right and reverse into the main road
- [ ] **B.** Make a U-turn in the main road
- [ ] **C.** Make a 'three-point' turn in the main road
- [x] **D.** Turn round in a side road

590 You may remove your seat belt when carrying out a manoeuvre that involves

Mark one answer
- [x] **A.** reversing
- [ ] **B.** a hill start
- [ ] **C.** an emergency stop
- [ ] **D.** driving slowly

591 You must not reverse

Mark one answer
- [x] **A.** for longer than necessary
- [ ] **B.** for more than a car's length
- [ ] **C.** into a side road
- [ ] **D.** in a built-up area

592 You are parked in a busy high street. What is the safest way to turn your vehicle around to go the opposite way?

Mark one answer
- [x] **A.** Find a quiet side road to turn round in
- [ ] **B.** Drive into a side road and reverse into the main road
- [ ] **C.** Get someone to stop the traffic
- [ ] **D.** Do a U-turn

593 When you are NOT sure that it is safe to reverse your vehicle you should

Mark one answer
- [ ] **A.** use your horn
- [ ] **B.** rev your engine
- [x] **C.** get out and check
- [ ] **D.** reverse slowly

594 When may you reverse from a side road into a main road?

Mark one answer
- [ ] **A.** Only if both roads are clear of traffic
- [x] **B.** Not at any time
- [ ] **C.** At any time
- [ ] **D.** Only if the main road is clear of traffic

595 You want to turn right at a box junction. There is oncoming traffic. You should

Mark one answer
- [x] **A.** wait in the box junction if your exit is cle
- [ ] **B.** wait before the junction until it is clear o all traffic
- [ ] **C.** drive on, you cannot turn right at a box junction
- [ ] **D.** drive slowly into the box junction when signalled by oncoming traffic

596 You are reversing your vehicle into side road. When would the greatest hazard to passing traffic occur?

Mark one answer
- [ ] **A.** After you've completed the manoeuvre
- [ ] **B.** Just before you actually begin to manoeuvre
- [ ] **C.** After you've entered the side road
- [x] **D.** When the front of your vehicle swings ou

597 You are driving on a road that has a cycle lane. The lane is marked by a broken white line. This means that

Mark two answers

- A. you should not drive in the lane unless it is unavoidable
- B. you should not park in the lane unless it is unavoidable
- C. you can drive in the lane at any time
- D. the lane must be used by motorcyclists in heavy traffic

598 When leaving your car unattended for a few minutes you should

Mark one answer

- A. leave the engine running
- B. switch the engine off but leave the key in
- C. lock it and remove the key
- D. park near a traffic warden

599 When parking and leaving your car for a few minutes you should

Mark one answer

- A. leave it unlocked
- B. lock it and remove the key
- C. leave the hazard warning lights on
- D. leave the interior light on

600 When leaving your car to help keep it secure you should

Mark one answer

- A. leave the hazard warning lights on
- B. lock it and remove the key
- C. park on a one-way street
- D. park in a residential area

601 When leaving your vehicle where should you park if possible?

Mark one answer

- A. Opposite a traffic island
- B. In a secure car park ✓
- C. On a bend
- D. At or near a taxi rank

602 Where is the safest place to park your vehicle at night?

Mark one answer

- A. In a garage ✓
- B. On a busy road
- C. In a quiet car park
- D. Near a red route

603 You are away from home and have to park your vehicle overnight. Where should you leave it?

Mark one answer

- A. Opposite another parked vehicle
- B. In a quiet road
- C. Opposite a traffic island
- D. In a secure car park ✓

604 To help keep your vehicle secure at night where should you park?

Mark one answer

- A. Near a police station
- B. In a quiet road
- C. On a red route
- D. In a well-lit area ✓

605 You are in the right-hand lane of a dual carriageway. You see signs showing that the right lane is closed 800 yards ahead. You should

Mark one answer

- [ ] **A.** keep in that lane until you reach the queue
- [ ] **B.** move to the left immediately
- [ ] **C.** wait and see which lane is moving faster
- [✓] **D.** move to the left in good time

606 You are leaving your vehicle parked on a road. When may you leave the engine running?

Mark one answer

- [ ] **A.** If you will be parked for less than five minutes
- [ ] **B.** If the battery is flat
- [ ] **C.** When in a 20mph zone
- [✓] **D.** Not on any occasion

607 You are driving on an urban clearw You may stop only to

Mark one answer

- [✓] **A.** set down and pick up passengers
- [ ] **B.** use a mobile telephone
- [ ] **C.** ask for directions
- [ ] **D.** load or unload goods

608 You are looking for somewhere to park your vehicle. The area is full EXCEPT for spaces marked 'disabl• use'. You can

Mark one answer

- [ ] **A.** use these spaces when elsewhere is full
- [ ] **B.** park if you stay with your vehicle
- [ ] **C.** use these spaces, disabled or not
- [✓] **D.** not park there unless permitted

609 Your vehicle is parked on the road night. When must you use sidelight

Mark one answer

- [ ] **A.** Where there are continuous white lines the middle of the road
- [✓] **B.** Where the speed limit exceeds 30mph
- [ ] **C.** Where you are facing oncoming traffic
- [ ] **D.** Where you are near a bus stop

510 On which THREE occasions MUST you stop your vehicle?

Mark three answers

- ☑ **A.** When involved in an accident
- ☑ **B.** At a red traffic light
- ☑ **C.** When signalled to do so by a police officer
- ☐ **D.** At a junction with double broken white lines
- ☐ **E.** At a pelican crossing when the amber light is flashing and no pedestrians are crossing

511 You are on a road that is only wide enough for one vehicle. There is a car coming towards you. What should you do?

Mark one answer

- ☐ **A.** Pull into a passing place on your right
- ☐ **B.** Force the other driver to reverse
- ☐ **C.** Pull into a passing place if your vehicle is wider
- ☑ **D.** Pull into a passing place on your left

612 What MUST you have to park in a disabled space?

Mark one answer

- ☑ **A.** An orange or blue badge
- ☐ **B.** A wheelchair
- ☐ **C.** An advanced driver certificate
- ☐ **D.** A modified vehicle

613 You are driving at night with full beam headlights on. A vehicle is overtaking you. You should dip your lights

Mark one answer

- ☐ **A.** some time after the vehicle has passed you
- ☐ **B.** before the vehicle starts to pass you
- ☐ **C.** only if the other driver dips their headlights
- ☑ **D.** as soon as the vehicle passes you

614 You MUST obey signs giving orders. These signs are mostly in

Mark one answer
- A. green rectangles
- B. red triangles
- C. blue rectangles
- ☑ D. red circles

615 Traffic signs giving orders are generally which shape?

Mark one answer
- A.
- B.
- C.
- ☑ D.

616 Which type of sign tells you NOT to do something?

Mark one answer
- ☑ A.
- B.
- C.
- D.

617 What does this sign mean?

20 ZONE
symbol
Place Name

Mark one answer
- ☑ A. Maximum speed limit with traffic calming
- B. Minimum speed limit with traffic calming
- C. '20 cars only' parking zone
- D. Only 20 cars allowed at any one time

618 Which sign means no motor vehicles are allowed?

Mark one answer
- A.
- ☑ B.
- C.
- D.

619 Which of these signs means no motor vehicles?

Mark one answer

A.

B.

C.

D.

620 What does this sign mean?

Mark one answer

A. New speed limit 20mph

B. No vehicles over 30 tonnes

C. Minimum speed limit 30mph

D. End of 20mph zone

621 What does this sign mean?

Mark one answer

A. No overtaking

B. No motor vehicles

C. Clearway (no stopping)

D. Cars and motorcycles only

622 What does this sign mean?

Mark one answer

A. No parking B. No road markings

C. No through road D. No entry

623 What does this sign mean?

Mark one answer

A. Bend to the right

B. Road on the right closed

C. No traffic from the right

D. No right turn

624 Which sign means 'no entry'?

Mark one answer

A.

B.

C.

D. ☑

627 Which sign means NO motor vehicle allowed?

Mark one answer

A.

B. ☑

C.

D.

625 What does this sign mean?

Mark one answer

- ☑ **A.** Route for trams only
- **B.** Route for buses only
- **C.** Parking for buses only
- **D.** Parking for trams only

628 What does this sign mean?

Mark one answer

- **A.** You have priority
- **B.** No motor vehicles
- **C.** Two-way traffic
- ☑ **D.** No overtaking

626 Which type of vehicle does this sign apply to?

Mark one answer

- **A.** Wide vehicles
- **B.** Long vehicles
- ☑ **C.** High vehicles
- **D.** Heavy vehicles

629 What does this sign mean?

Mark one answer

- **A.** Keep in one lane
- **B.** Give way to oncoming traffic
- ☑ **C.** Do not overtake
- **D.** Form two lanes

630 Which sign means no overtaking?

Mark one answer

A.

B.

C.

D.

631 What does this sign mean?

Mark one answer

A. Waiting restrictions apply

B. Waiting permitted

C. National speed limit applies

D. Clearway (no stopping)

632 What does this sign mean?

URBAN CLEARWAY	
Monday to Friday	
am	pm
8.00 - 9.30	4.30 - 6.30

Mark one answer

A. You can park on the days and times shown

B. No parking on the days and times shown

C. No parking at all from Monday to Friday

D. You can park at any time; the urban clearway ends

633 What does this sign mean?

Zone
ENDS

Mark one answer

A. End of restricted speed area

B. End of restricted parking area

C. End of clearway

D. End of cycle route

634 Which sign means 'no stopping'?

Mark one answer

A.

B.

C.

D.

635 What does this sign mean?

Mark one answer

A. Roundabout

B. Crossroads

C. No stopping

D. No entry

636 You see this sign ahead. It means

Mark one answer
- [ ] **A.** national speed limit applies
- [ ] **B.** waiting restrictions apply
- [x] **C.** no stopping
- [ ] **D.** no entry

637 What does this sign mean?

Mark one answer
- [x] **A.** Distance to parking place ahead
- [ ] **B.** Distance to public telephone ahead
- [ ] **C.** Distance to public house ahead
- [ ] **D.** Distance to passing place ahead

638 What does this sign mean?

Mark one answer
- [ ] **A.** Vehicles may not park on the verge or footway
- [ ] **B.** Vehicles may park on the left-hand side of the road only
- [x] **C.** Vehicles may park fully on the verge or footway
- [ ] **D.** Vehicles may park on the right-hand side of the road only

639 What does this traffic sign mean?

Mark one answer
- [ ] **A.** No overtaking allowed
- [x] **B.** Give priority to oncoming traffic
- [ ] **C.** Two-way traffic
- [ ] **D.** One-way traffic only

640 What is the meaning of this traffic sign?

Mark one answer
- [ ] **A.** End of two-way road
- [ ] **B.** Give priority to vehicles coming towards you
- [x] **C.** You have priority over vehicles coming towards you
- [ ] **D.** Bus lane ahead

641 Which sign means 'traffic has priority over oncoming vehicles'?

Mark one answer
- [ ] **A.**
- [ ] **B.**
- [x] **C.**
- [ ] **D.**

642 What MUST you do when you see this sign?

Mark one answer

- [ ] **A.** Stop, ONLY if traffic is approaching
- [✓] **B.** Stop, even if the road is clear
- [ ] **C.** Stop, ONLY if children are waiting
- [ ] **D.** Stop, ONLY if a red light is showing

STOP

643 What does this sign mean?

Mark one answer

- [ ] **A.** No overtaking
- [ ] **B.** You are entering a one-way street
- [ ] **C.** Two-way traffic ahead
- [✓] **D.** You have priority over vehicles from the opposite direction

644 What shape is a STOP sign at a junction?

Mark one answer

- [ ] **A.**
- [ ] **B.**
- [ ] **C.**
- [✓] **D.**

645 At a junction you see this sign partly covered by snow. What does it mean?

Mark one answer

- [ ] **A.** Crossroads
- [ ] **B.** Give way
- [✓] **C.** Stop
- [ ] **D.** Turn right

646 Which shape is used for a GIVE WAY sign?

Mark one answer

- [ ] **A.**
- [ ] **B.**
- [ ] **C.**
- [✓] **D.**

647 What does this sign mean?

Mark one answer

- [ ] **A.** Service area 30 miles ahead
- [ ] **B.** Maximum speed 30mph
- [✓] **C.** Minimum speed 30mph
- [ ] **D.** Lay-by 30 miles ahead

648 Which of these signs means turn left ahead ?

Mark one answer

A.

B. ☑

C.

D.

649 What does this sign mean?

Mark one answer

A. Buses turning
B. Ring road
C. ☑ Mini-roundabout
D. Keep right

650 What does this sign mean?

Mark one answer

A. Give way to oncoming vehicles
B. Approaching traffic passes you on both sides
C. Turn off at the next available junction
D. ☑ Pass either side to get to the same destination

651 What does this sign mean?

Mark one answer

A. ☑ Route for trams
B. Give way to trams
C. Route for buses
D. Give way to buses

Only

652 What does a circular traffic sign wit a blue background do?

Mark one answer

A. Give warning of a motorway ahead
B. Give directions to a car park
C. Give motorway information
D. ☑ Give an instruction

653 Which of these signs means that yo are entering a one-way street?

Mark one answer

A.

B. ☑

C.

D.

654 Where would you see a contraflow bus and cycle lane?

Mark one answer

A. On a dual carriageway
B. On a roundabout
C. On an urban motorway
D. ☑ On a one-way street

655 What does this sign mean?

Mark one answer
- A. Bus station on the right
- ✓ B. Contraflow bus lane
- C. With-flow bus lane
- D. Give way to buses

656 What does this sign mean?

Mark one answer
- ✓ A. With-flow bus and cycle lane
- B. Contraflow bus and cycle lane
- C. No buses and cycles allowed
- D. No waiting for buses and cycles

657 What does a sign with a brown background show?

Mark one answer
- ✓ A. Tourist directions
- B. Primary roads
- C. Motorway routes
- D. Minor routes

658 This sign means

Mark one answer
- ✓ A. tourist attraction
- B. beware of trains
- C. level crossing
- D. beware of trams

659 What are triangular signs for?

Mark one answer
- ✓ A. To give warnings
- B. To give information
- C. To give orders
- D. To give directions

660 What does this sign mean?

Mark one answer
- A. Turn left ahead
- ✓ B. T-junction
- C. No through road
- D. Give way

661 What does this sign mean?

Mark one answer
- A. Multi-exit roundabout
- ✓ B. Risk of ice
- C. Six roads converge
- D. Place of historical interest

662 What does this sign mean?

Mark one answer
- ☑ **A.** Crossroads
- ☐ **B.** Level crossing with gate
- ☐ **C.** Level crossing without gate
- ☐ **D.** Ahead only

663 What does this sign mean?

Mark one answer
- ☐ **A.** Ring road
- ☐ **B.** Mini-roundabout
- ☐ **C.** No vehicles
- ☑ **D.** Roundabout

664 Which FOUR of these would be indicated by a triangular road sign?

Mark four answers
- ☑ **A.** Road narrows
- ☐ **B.** Ahead only
- ☑ **C.** Low bridge
- ☐ **D.** Minimum speed
- ☑ **E.** Children crossing
- ☑ **F.** T-junction

665 What does this sign mean?

Mark one answer
- ☐ **A.** Cyclists must dismount
- ☐ **B.** Cycles are not allowed
- ☑ **C.** Cycle route ahead
- ☐ **D.** Cycle in single file

666 Which sign means that pedestrians may be walking along the road?

Mark one answer
- ☑ **A.**
- ☐ **B.**
- ☐ **C.**
- ☐ **D.**

667 Which of these signs warn you of a pedestrian crossing?

Mark one answer
- ☑ **A.**
- ☐ **B.**
- ☐ **C.**
- ☐ **D.**

668 What does this sign mean?

Mark one answer
- ☐ **A.** No footpath ahead
- ☐ **B.** Pedestrians only ahead
- ☑ **C.** Pedestrian crossing ahead
- ☐ **D.** School crossing ahead

669 What does this sign mean?

Mark one answer
- [ ] **A.** School crossing patrol
- [ ] **B.** No pedestrians allowed
- [ ] **C.** Pedestrian zone – no vehicles
- [x] **D.** Pedestrian crossing ahead

670 Which of these signs means there is a double bend ahead?

Mark one answer
- [ ] **A.**

- [x] **B.**

- [ ] **C.**

- [ ] **D.**

671 What does this sign mean?

Mark one answer
- [ ] **A.** Wait at the barriers
- [ ] **B.** Wait at the crossroads
- [x] **C.** Give way to trams
- [ ] **D.** Give way to farm vehicles

672 What does this sign mean?

Mark one answer
- [ ] **A.** Humpback bridge
- [x] **B.** Humps in the road
- [ ] **C.** Entrance to tunnel
- [ ] **D.** Soft verges

673 What does this sign mean?

Mark one answer
- [ ] **A.** Low bridge ahead
- [x] **B.** Tunnel ahead
- [ ] **C.** Ancient monument ahead
- [ ] **D.** Accident black spot ahead

674 What does this sign mean?

Mark one answer
- [ ] **A.** Two-way traffic straight ahead
- [x] **B.** Two-way traffic crossing a one-way street
- [ ] **C.** Two-way traffic over a bridge
- [ ] **D.** Two-way traffic crosses a two-way road

675 Which sign means 'two-way traffic crosses a one-way road'?

Mark one answer

A.

☑ B.

C.

D.

676 Which of these signs means the end of a dual carriageway?

Mark one answer

A.

B.

C.

☑ D.

677 What does this sign mean?

Mark one answer

☑ A. End of dual carriageway

B. Tall bridge

C. Road narrows

D. End of narrow bridge

678 What does this sign mean?

Mark one answer

A. Two-way traffic ahead across a one-way street

B. Traffic approaching you has priority

☑ C. Two-way traffic straight ahead

D. Motorway contraflow system ahead

679 What does this sign mean?

Mark one answer

☑ A. Crosswinds

B. Road noise

C. Airport

D. Adverse camber

680 What does this traffic sign mean?

Mark one answer

A. Slippery road ahead

B. Tyres liable to punctures ahead

☑ C. Danger ahead

D. Service area ahead

681 You are about to overtake when you see this sign. You should

Mark one answer

- [ ] **A.** overtake the other driver as quickly as possible
- [ ] **B.** move to the right to get a better view
- [ ] **C.** switch your headlights on before overtaking
- [x] **D.** hold back until you can see clearly ahead

Hidden dip

682 What does this sign mean?

Mark one answer

- [ ] **A.** Level crossing with gate or barrier
- [ ] **B.** Gated road ahead
- [ ] **C.** Level crossing without gate or barrier
- [ ] **D.** Cattle grid ahead

683 What does this sign mean?

Mark one answer

- [ ] **A.** No trams ahead
- [ ] **B.** Oncoming trams
- [ ] **C.** Trams crossing ahead
- [ ] **D.** Trams only

684 What does this sign mean?

Mark one answer

- [ ] **A.** Adverse camber
- [x] **B.** Steep hill downwards
- [ ] **C.** Uneven road
- [ ] **D.** Steep hill upwards

685 What does this sign mean?

Mark one answer

- [x] **A.** Quayside or river bank
- [ ] **B.** Steep hill downwards
- [ ] **C.** Slippery road
- [ ] **D.** Road liable to flooding

686 What does this sign mean?

Mark one answer

- [ ] **A.** Uneven road surface
- [ ] **B.** Bridge over the road
- [ ] **C.** Road ahead ends
- [x] **D.** Water across the road

Ford

687 What does this sign mean?

Mark one answer

- [x] **A.** Humpback bridge
- [ ] **B.** Traffic calming hump
- [ ] **C.** Low bridge
- [ ] **D.** Uneven road

688 What does this sign mean?

Mark one answer
- [ ] **A.** Turn left for parking area
- [x] **B.** No through road on the left
- [ ] **C.** No entry for traffic turning left
- [ ] **D.** Turn left for ferry terminal

689 What does this sign mean?

Mark one answer
- [ ] **A.** T-junction
- [x] **B.** No through road
- [ ] **C.** Telephone box ahead
- [ ] **D.** Toilet ahead

690 Which sign means 'no through road'?

Mark one answer
- [ ] **A.**
- [ ] **B.**
- [x] **C.**
- [ ] **D.**

691 Which of the following signs inform you that you are coming to a No Through Road ?

Mark one answer
- [ ] **A.**
- [ ] **B.**
- [x] **C.**
- [ ] **D.**

692 What does this sign mean?

Mark one answer
- [x] **A.** Direction to park and ride car park
- [ ] **B.** No parking for buses or coaches
- [ ] **C.** Directions to bus and coach park
- [ ] **D.** Parking area for cars and coaches

693 You are going through a tunnel and you see this sign. What does it mean?

Mark one answer
- [x] **A.** Direction to emergency pedestrian exit
- [ ] **B.** Beware of pedestrians, no footpath ahead
- [ ] **C.** No access for pedestrians
- [ ] **D.** Beware of pedestrians crossing ahead

694 Which is the sign for a ring road?

Mark one answer

A.

B.

C.

D.

695 What does this sign mean?

Mark one answer

A. Route for lorries
B. Ring road
C. Rest area
D. Roundabout

696 What does this sign mean?

Mark one answer

A. Hilly road
B. Humps in road
C. Holiday route
D. Hospital route

697 What does this sign mean?

Mark one answer

A. The right-hand lane ahead is narrow
B. Right-hand lane for buses only
C. Right-hand lane for turning right
D. The right-hand lane is closed ✓

698 What does this sign mean?

Mark one answer

A. Change to the left lane
B. Leave at the next exit
C. Contraflow system ✓
D. One-way street

699 To avoid an accident when entering a contraflow system, you should

Mark three answers

A. reduce speed in good time ✓
B. switch lanes any time to make progress
C. choose an appropriate lane early ✓
D. keep the correct separation distance ✓
E. increase speed to pass through quickly
F. follow other motorists closely to avoid long queues

700 What does this sign mean?

Mark one answer

- [ ] **A.** Leave motorway at next exit
- [✓] **B.** Lane for heavy and slow vehicles
- [ ] **C.** All lorries use the hard shoulder
- [ ] **D.** Rest area for lorries

701 You see this traffic light ahead. Which light(s) will come on next?

Mark one answer

- [✓] **A.** Red alone
- [ ] **B.** Red and amber together
- [ ] **C.** Green and amber together
- [ ] **D.** Green alone

702 You are approaching a red traffic light. The signal will change from red to

Mark one answer

- [✓] **A.** red and amber, then green
- [ ] **B.** green, then amber
- [ ] **C.** amber, then green
- [ ] **D.** green and amber, then green

703 A red traffic light means

Mark one answer

- [ ] **A.** you should stop unless turning left
- [ ] **B.** stop, if you are able to brake safely
- [✓] **C.** you must stop and wait behind the stop line
- [ ] **D.** proceed with caution

704 At traffic lights, amber on its own means

Mark one answer

- [ ] **A.** prepare to go
- [ ] **B.** go if the way is clear
- [ ] **C.** go if no pedestrians are crossing
- [✓] **D.** stop at the stop line

705 You are approaching traffic lights. Red and amber are showing. This means

Mark one answer

- [ ] **A.** pass the lights if the road is clear
- [ ] **B.** there is a fault with the lights – take care
- [✓] **C.** wait for the green light before you pass the lights
- [ ] **D.** the lights are about to change to red

06 You are at a junction controlled by traffic lights. When should you NOT proceed at green?

rk one answer

- **A.** When pedestrians are waiting to cross
- **B.** When your exit from the junction is blocked
- **C.** When you think the lights may be about to change
- **D.** When you intend to turn right

07 You are in the left-hand lane at traffic lights. You are waiting to turn left. At which of these traffic lights must you NOT move on?

rk one answer

A.   B.

C.   D.

08 What does this sign mean?

rk one answer

- **A.** Traffic lights out of order
- **B.** Amber signal out of order
- **C.** Temporary traffic lights ahead
- **D.** New traffic lights ahead

709 When traffic lights are out of order, who has priority?

Mark one answer

- **A.** Traffic going straight on
- **B.** Traffic turning right
- **C.** Nobody ✓
- **D.** Traffic turning left

710 These flashing red lights mean STOP. In which THREE of the following places could you find them?

Mark three answers

- **A.** Pelican crossings
- **B.** Lifting bridges ✓
- **C.** Zebra crossings
- **D.** Level crossings ✓
- **E.** Motorway exits
- **F.** Fire stations ✓

711 What do these zig zag lines at pedestrian crossings mean?

Mark one answer

- **A.** No parking at any time ✓
- **B.** Parking allowed only for a short time
- **C.** Slow down to 20mph
- **D.** Sounding horns is not allowed

712
The white line painted in the centre of the road means

Mark one answer

- **A.** the area is hazardous and you must not overtake
- **B.** you should give priority to oncoming vehicles
- ☑ **C.** do not cross the line unless the road ahead is clear
- **D.** the area is a national speed limit zone

713
When may you cross a double solid white line in the middle of the road?

Mark one answer

- **A.** To pass traffic that is queuing back at a junction
- **B.** To pass a car signalling to turn left ahead
- ☑ **C.** To pass a road maintenance vehicle travelling at 10mph or less
- **D.** To pass a vehicle that is towing a trailer

714
A white line like this along the ce of the road is a

Mark one answer

- **A.** bus lane marking
- ☑ **B.** hazard warning
- **C.** 'give way' marking
- **D.** lane marking

715
What does this road marking mea

Mark one answer

- **A.** Do not cross the line
- **B.** No stopping allowed
- ☑ **C.** You are approaching a hazard
- **D.** No overtaking allowed

716
This marking appears on the road just before a

Mark one answer

- **A.** no entry sign
- ☑ **B.** give way sign
- **C.** stop sign
- **D.** no through road sign

717 Where would you see this road marking?

ark one answer
- **A.** At traffic lights
- **B.** On road humps
- **C.** Near a level crossing
- **D.** At a box junction

718 Which is a hazard warning line?

ark one answer
- **A.**

- **B.**

- **C.**

- **D.**

719 At this junction there is a stop sign with a solid white line on the road surface. Why is there a stop sign here?

Mark one answer
- **A.** Speed on the major road is de-restricted
- **B.** It is a busy junction
- ☑ **C.** Visibility along the major road is restricted
- **D.** There are hazard warning lines in the centre of the road

720 You see this line across the road at the entrance to a roundabout. What does it mean?

Mark one answer
- ☑ **A.** Give way to traffic from the right
- **B.** Traffic from the left has right of way
- **C.** You have right of way
- **D.** Stop at the line

721 Where would you find this road marking?

Mark one answer
- [ ] **A.** At a railway crossing
- [x] **B.** At a junction
- [ ] **C.** On a motorway
- [ ] **D.** On a pedestrian crossing

722 How will a police officer in a patrol vehicle normally get you to stop?

Mark one answer
- [x] **A.** Flash the headlights, indicate left and point to the left
- [ ] **B.** Wait until you stop, then approach you
- [ ] **C.** Use the siren, overtake, cut in front and stop
- [ ] **D.** Pull alongside you, use the siren and wave you to stop

723 There is a police car following you. The police officer flashes the headlights and points to the left. What should you do?

Mark one answer
- [ ] **A.** Turn at the next left
- [x] **B.** Pull up on the left
- [ ] **C.** Stop immediately
- [ ] **D.** Move over to the left

724 You approach a junction. The traffic lights are not working. A police officer gives this signal. You should

Mark one answer
- [ ] **A.** turn left only
- [ ] **B.** turn right only
- [ ] **C.** stop level with the officer's arm
- [x] **D.** stop at the stop line

725 The driver of the car in front is giving this arm signal. What does it mean

Mark one answer
- [ ] **A.** The driver is slowing down
- [ ] **B.** The driver intends to turn right
- [ ] **C.** The driver wishes to overtake
- [x] **D.** The driver intends to turn left

726 Why should you make sure that you have cancelled your indicators after turning?

Mark one answer
- [ ] **A.** To avoid flattening the battery
- [x] **B.** To avoid misleading other road users
- [ ] **C.** To avoid dazzling other road users
- [ ] **D.** To avoid damage to the indicator relay

27 Where would you see these road markings?

Mark one answer

- A. At a level crossing
- B. On a motorway slip road
- C. At a pedestrian crossing
- D. On a single-track road

28 When may you NOT overtake on the left?

Mark one answer

- A. On a free-flowing motorway or dual carriageway
- B. When the traffic is moving slowly in queues
- C. On a one-way street
- D. When the car in front is signalling to turn right

29 What does this motorway sign mean?

Mark one answer

- A. Change to the lane on your left
- B. Leave the motorway at the next exit
- C. Change to the opposite carriageway
- D. Pull up on the hard shoulder

730 What does this motorway sign mean?

Mark one answer

- A. Temporary minimum speed 50mph
- B. No services for 50 miles
- C. Obstruction 50 metres (164 feet) ahead
- [✓] D. Temporary maximum speed 50mph

731 What does this sign mean?

Mark one answer

- A. Through traffic to use left lane
- B. Right-hand lane T-junction only
- [✓] C. Right-hand lane closed ahead
- D. 11 tonne weight limit

732 On a motorway this sign means

Mark one answer

- A. move over onto the hard shoulder
- B. overtaking on the left only
- C. leave the motorway at the next exit
- [✓] D. move to the lane on your left

733
What does '25' mean on this motorway sign?

Nottingham
A46
25

Mark one answer
- A. The distance to the nearest town
- B. The route number of the road
- ☑ C. The number of the next junction
- D. The speed limit on the slip road

734
The right-hand lane of a three-lane motorway is

Mark one answer
- A. for lorries only
- ☑ B. an overtaking lane
- C. the right-turn lane
- D. an acceleration lane

735
Where can you find reflective amber studs on a motorway?

Mark one answer
- A. Separating the slip road from the motorway
- B. On the left-hand edge of the road
- ☑ C. On the right-hand edge of the road
- D. Separating the lanes

736
Where on a motorway would you green reflective studs?

Mark one answer
- A. Separating driving lanes
- B. Between the hard shoulder and the carriageway
- ☑ C. At slip road entrances and exits
- D. Between the carriageway and the centr. reservation

737
You are travelling along a motorw You see this sign. You should

Mark one answer
- ☑ A. leave the motorway at the next exit
- B. turn left immediately
- C. change lane
- D. move onto the hard shoulder

738
You see these signs overhead on motorway. They mean

Mark one answer
- ☑ A. leave the motorway at the next exit
- B. all vehicles use the hard shoulder
- C. sharp bend to the left ahead
- D. stop, all lanes ahead closed

739 What does this sign mean?

Mark one answer

A. No motor vehicles ☑ B. End of motorway
C. No through road ☐ D. End of bus lane

740 Which of these signs means that the national speed limit applies?

Mark one answer

A.

☐ B.

C.

☑ D.

741 What is the maximum speed on a single carriageway road?

Mark one answer

A. 50mph
B. 60mph
C. 40mph
D. 70mph

742 What does this sign mean?

Mark one answer

☐ A. End of motorway
☑ B. End of restriction
☐ C. Lane ends ahead
☑ D. Free recovery ends

743 This sign is advising you to

Mark one answer

☑ A. follow the route diversion
☐ B. follow the signs to the picnic area
☐ C. give way to pedestrians
☐ D. give way to cyclists

744 Why would this temporary speed limit sign be shown?

Mark one answer

☐ A. To warn of the end of the motorway
☐ B. To warn you of a low bridge
☐ C. To warn you of a junction ahead
☑ D. To warn of road works ahead

745 This traffic sign means there is

Mark one answer

- ☑ **A.** a compulsory maximum speed limit
- ☐ **B.** an advisory maximum speed limit
- ☐ **C.** a compulsory minimum speed limit
- ☐ **D.** an advised separation distance

746 You see this sign at a crossroads. You should

Mark one answer

- ☐ **A.** maintain the same speed
- ☑ **B.** carry on with great care
- ☐ **C.** find another route
- ☐ **D.** telephone the police

747 You are signalling to turn right in busy traffic. How would you confirm your intention safely?

Mark one answer

- ☐ **A.** Sound the horn
- ☑ **B.** Give an arm signal
- ☐ **C.** Flash your headlights
- ☐ **D.** Position over the centre line

748 What does this sign mean?

Mark one answer

- ☐ **A.** Motorcycles only
- ☐ **B.** No cars
- ☐ **C.** Cars only
- ☑ **D.** No motorcycles

749 You are on a motorway. You see ⬧ sign on a lorry that has stopped the right-hand lane. You should

Mark one answer

- ☐ **A.** move into the right-hand lane
- ☐ **B.** stop behind the flashing lights
- ☑ **C.** pass the lorry on the left
- ☐ **D.** leave the motorway at the next exit

750 You are on a motorway. Red flas⬧ lights appear above your lane or What should you do?

Mark one answer

- ☐ **A.** Continue in that lane and look for fur⬧ information
- ☑ **B.** Move into another lane in good time
- ☐ **C.** Pull onto the hard shoulder
- ☐ **D.** Stop and wait for an instruction to pro⬧

751 A red traffic light means

Mark one answer

A. you must stop behind the white stop line

B. you may go straight on if there is no other traffic

C. you may turn left if it is safe to do so

D. you must slow down and prepare to stop if traffic has started to cross

752 The driver of this car is giving an arm signal. What are they about to do?

Mark one answer

A. Turn to the right

B. Turn to the left

C. Go straight ahead

D. Let pedestrians cross

753 Which arm signal tells you that the car you are following is going to turn left?

Mark one answer

A.

B.

C.

D.

754 When may you sound the horn?

Mark one answer

A. To give you right of way

B. To attract a friend's attention

C. To warn others of your presence

D. To make slower drivers move over

755 You must not use your horn when you are stationary

Mark one answer

A. unless a moving vehicle may cause you danger

B. at any time whatsoever

C. unless it is used only briefly

D. except for signalling that you have just arrived

756 You are approaching a zebra crossing where pedestrians are waiting. Which arm signal might you give?

Mark one answer

A.

B.

C.

D.

757 The white line along the side of the road

Mark one answer

- A. shows the edge of the carriageway
- B. shows the approach to a hazard
- C. means no parking
- D. means no overtaking

758 You see this white arrow on the road ahead. It means

Mark one answer

- A. entrance on the left
- B. all vehicles turn left
- C. keep left of the hatched markings
- D. road bending to the left

759 How should you give an arm signal turn left?

Mark one answer

- A.
- B.
- C.
- D.

760 You are waiting at a T-junction. A vehicle is coming from the right with the left signal flashing. What should you do?

Mark one answer

- A. Move out and accelerate hard
- B. Wait until the vehicle starts to turn in
- C. Pull out before the vehicle reaches the junction
- D. Move out slowly

761 When may you use hazard warning lights when driving?

Mark one answer

- [ ] **A.** Instead of sounding the horn in a built-up area between 11.30pm and 7am
- [x] **B.** On a motorway or unrestricted dual carriageway, to warn of a hazard ahead
- [ ] **C.** On rural routes, after a warning sign of animals
- [ ] **D.** On the approach to toucan crossings where cyclists are waiting to cross

762 You are driving on a motorway. There is a slow-moving vehicle ahead. On the back you see this sign. You should

Mark one answer

- [ ] **A.** pass on the right
- [ ] **B.** pass on the left
- [ ] **C.** leave at the next exit
- [ ] **D.** drive no further

763 You should NOT normally stop on these markings near schools

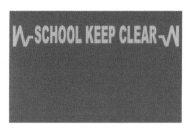

Mark one answer

- [ ] **A.** except when picking up children
- [x] **B.** under any circumstances
- [ ] **C.** unless there is nowhere else available
- [ ] **D.** except to set down children

764 When other drivers flash their headlights at you it means

Mark one answer

- [ ] **A.** that there is a radar speed trap ahead
- [ ] **B.** that they are giving way to you
- [x] **C.** that they are warning you of their presence
- [ ] **D.** that there is something wrong with your vehicle

765 To drive on the road learners MUST

Mark one answer

- [ ] **A.** have NO penalty points on their licence
- [ ] **B.** have taken professional instruction
- [x] **C.** have a signed, valid provisional licence
- [ ] **D.** apply for a driving test within 12 months

766 Before driving anyone else's motor vehicle you should make sure that

Mark one answer

- [ ] **A.** the vehicle owner has third party insurance cover
- [ ] **B.** your own vehicle has insurance cover
- [x] **C.** the vehicle is insured for your use
- [ ] **D.** the owner has left the insurance documents in the vehicle

767 Your car needs an MOT certificate. If you drive without one this could invalidate your

Mark one answer

- [ ] **A.** vehicle service record
- [x] **B.** insurance
- [ ] **C.** road tax disc
- [ ] **D.** vehicle registration document

768 When is it legal to drive a car over three years old without an MOT certificate?

Mark one answer

- [ ] **A.** Up to seven days after the old certificate has run out
- [ ] **B.** When driving to an MOT centre to arrange an appointment
- [ ] **C.** Just after buying a secondhand car with MOT
- [x] **D.** When driving to an appointment at an MOT centre

769 To supervise a learner driver you must

Mark two answers

- [x] **A.** have held a full licence for at least 3 years
- [x] **B.** be at least 21
- [ ] **C.** be an approved driving instructor
- [ ] **D.** hold an advanced driving certificate

770 The cost of your insurance may be reduced if

Mark one answer

- [ ] **A.** your car is large and powerful
- [ ] **B.** you are using the car for work purposes
- [ ] **C.** you have penalty points on your licence
- [x] **D.** you are over 25 years old

771 The cost of your insurance may be reduced if you

Mark two answers

- A. are over 25 years old
- B. are under 25 years old
- C. do not wear glasses
- D. pass the driving test first time
- E. complete the Pass Plus scheme

772 How old must you be to supervise a learner driver?

Mark one answer

- A. 18 years old
- B. 19 years old
- C. 20 years old
- D. 21 years old

773 A newly qualified driver must

Mark one answer

- A. display green 'L' plates
- B. not exceed 40mph for 12 months
- C. be accompanied on a motorway
- D. have valid motor insurance

774 What is the legal minimum insurance cover you must have to drive on public roads?

Mark one answer

- A. Third party, fire and theft
- B. Fully comprehensive
- C. Third party only
- D. Personal injury cover

775 You have third party insurance. What does this cover?

Mark three answers

- A. Damage to your own vehicle
- B. Damage to your vehicle by fire
- ☑ C. Injury to another person
- ☑ D. Damage to someone's property
- ☑ E. Damage to other vehicles
- F. Injury to yourself

776 For which TWO of these must you show your motor insurance certificate?

Mark two answers

- A. When you are taking your driving test
- B. When buying or selling a vehicle
- ☑ C. When a police officer asks you for it
- ☑ D. When you are taxing your vehicle
- E. When having an MOT inspection

777 Vehicle excise duty is often called 'Road Tax' or 'The Tax Disc'. You must

Mark one answer

- A. keep it with your registration document
- ☑ B. display it clearly on your vehicle
- C. keep it concealed safely in your vehicle
- D. carry it on you at all times

778 Motor cars must FIRST have an MOT test certificate when they are

Mark one answer

- [ ] A. one year old
- [✓] B. three years old
- [ ] C. five years old
- [ ] D. seven years old

779 Your vehicle needs a current MOT certificate. You do not have one. Until you do have one you will not be able to renew your

Mark one answer

- [ ] A. driving licence
- [ ] B. vehicle insurance
- [✓] C. road tax disc
- [ ] D. vehicle registration document

780 Which THREE of the following do you need before you can drive legally?

Mark three answers

- [✓] A. A valid driving licence with a signature
- [✓] B. A valid tax disc displayed on your vehicle
- [ ] C. Proof of your identity
- [✓] D. Proper insurance cover
- [ ] E. Breakdown cover
- [ ] F. A vehicle handbook

781 Which THREE pieces of information are found on a vehicle registration document?

Mark three answers

- [✓] A. Registered keeper
- [✓] B. Make of the vehicle
- [ ] C. Service history details
- [ ] D. Date of the MOT
- [ ] E. Type of insurance cover
- [✓] F. Engine size

782 You have a duty to contact the licensing authority when

Mark three answers

- [ ] A. you go abroad on holiday
- [✓] B. you change your vehicle
- [✓] C. you change your name
- [ ] D. your job status is changed
- [✓] E. your permanent address changes
- [ ] F. your job involves travelling abroad

783 You must notify the licensing authority when

Mark three answers

- [✓] A. your health affects your driving
- [✓] B. your eyesight does not meet a set standard
- [ ] C. you intend lending your vehicle
- [ ] D. your vehicle requires an MOT certificate
- [✓] E. you change your vehicle

84 You have just bought a secondhand vehicle. When should you tell the licensing authority of change of ownership?

Mark one answer

- ☑ A. Immediately
- ☐ B. After 28 days
- ☐ C. When an MOT is due
- ☐ D. Only when you insure it

85 Your vehicle is insured third party only. This covers

Mark two answers

- ☐ A. damage to your vehicle
- ☐ B. damage to other vehicles
- ☐ C. injury to yourself
- ☐ D. injury to others
- ☐ E. all damage and injury

86 Your motor insurance policy has an excess of £100. What does this mean?

Mark one answer

- ☐ A. The insurance company will pay the first £100 of any claim
- ☐ B. You will be paid £100 if you do not have an accident
- ☐ C. Your vehicle is insured for a value of £100 if it is stolen
- ☐ D. You will have to pay the first £100 of any claim

787 You have just passed your practical driving test. Within two years you get six penalty points on your licence. You will have to

Mark two answers

- ☐ A. retake only your theory test
- ☑ B. retake your theory and practical tests
- ☐ C. retake only your practical test
- ☐ D. reapply for your full licence immediately
- ☑ E. reapply for your provisional licence

788 When you apply to renew your vehicle excise licence (tax disc) you must produce

Mark one answer

- ☑ A. a valid insurance certificate
- ☐ B. the old tax disc
- ☐ C. the vehicle handbook
- ☐ D. a valid driving licence

789 What is the legal minimum insurance cover you must have to drive on public roads?

Mark one answer

- ☐ A. Fire and theft
- ☐ B. Theft only
- ☑ C. Third party
- ☐ D. Fire only

790
An MOT certificate is normally valid for

Mark one answer
- [ ] **A.** three years after the date it was issued
- [ ] **B.** 10,000 miles
- [x] **C.** one year after the date it was issued
- [ ] **D.** 30,000 miles

791
A cover note is a document issued before you receive your

Mark one answer
- [ ] **A.** driving licence
- [x] **B.** insurance certificate
- [ ] **C.** registration document
- [ ] **D.** MOT certificate

792
A police officer asks to see your documents. You do not have them with you. You may produce them a police station within

Mark one answer
- [ ] **A.** five days
- [x] **B.** seven days
- [ ] **C.** 14 days
- [ ] **D.** 21 days

793
Which TWO of these are NOT requi to have an MOT certificate?

Mark two answers
- [ ] **A.** Motor cycle
- [x] **B.** Small trailer
- [ ] **C.** Ambulance
- [x] **D.** Caravan

794 While driving, a warning light on your vehicle's instrument panel comes on. You should

Mark one answer

- A. continue if the engine sounds alright
- B. hope that it is just a temporary electrical fault
- C. deal with the problem when there is more time
- D. check out the problem quickly and safely

795 You have broken down on a two-way road. You have a warning triangle. You should place the warning triangle at least how far from your vehicle?

Mark one answer

- A. 5 metres (16 feet)
- B. 25 metres (82 feet)
- C. 45 metres (147 feet)
- D. 100 metres (328 feet)

796 You break down on a level crossing. The lights have not yet begun to flash. Which THREE things should you do?

Mark three answers

- ☑ A. Telephone the signal operator
- ☑ B. Leave your vehicle and get everyone clear
- ☐ C. Walk down the track and signal the next train
- ☑ D. Move the vehicle if a signal operator tells you to
- ☐ E. Tell drivers behind what has happened

797 Your vehicle has broken down on an automatic railway level crossing. What should you do FIRST?

Mark one answer

- ☑ A. Get everyone out of the vehicle and clear of the crossing
- ☐ B. Phone the signal operator so that trains can be stopped
- ☐ C. Walk along the track to give warning to any approaching trains
- ☐ D. Try to push the vehicle clear of the crossing as soon as possible

798 Your tyre bursts while you are driving. Which TWO things should you do?

Mark two answers

- ☐ A. Pull on the handbrake
- ☐ B. Brake as quickly as possible
- ☑ C. Pull up slowly at the side of the road
- ☑ D. Hold the steering wheel firmly to keep control
- ☐ E. Continue on at a normal speed

799
Which TWO things should you do when a front tyre bursts?

Mark two answers
- [ ] A. Apply the handbrake to stop the vehicle
- [ ] B. Brake firmly and quickly
- [x] C. Let the vehicle roll to a stop
- [ ] D. Hold the steering wheel lightly
- [x] E. Grip the steering wheel firmly

800
Your vehicle has a puncture on a motorway. What should you do?

Mark one answer
- [ ] A. Drive slowly to the next service area to get assistance
- [ ] B. Pull up on the hard shoulder. Change the wheel as quickly as possible
- [x] C. Pull up on the hard shoulder. Use the emergency phone to get assistance
- [ ] D. Switch on your hazard lights. Stop in your lane

801
What TWO safeguards could you take against fire risk to your vehicle?

Mark two answers
- [ ] A. Keep water levels above maximum
- [x] B. Carry a fire extinguisher
- [ ] C. Avoid driving with a full tank of petrol
- [ ] D. Use unleaded petrol
- [x] E. Check out any strong smell of petrol
- [ ] F. Use low octane fuel

802
Which of these items should you carry in your vehicle for use in the event of an accident?

Mark three answers
- [ ] A. Road map
- [ ] B. Can of petrol
- [ ] C. Jump leads
- [x] D. Fire extinguisher
- [x] E. First Aid kit
- [x] F. Warning triangle

803
You are in an accident on a two-way road. You have a warning triangle with you. At what distance before obstruction should you place the warning triangle?

Mark one answer
- [ ] A. 25 metres (82 feet)
- [x] B. 45 metres (147 feet)
- [ ] C. 100 metres (328 feet)
- [ ] D. 150 metres (492 feet)

804
You have broken down on a two-way road. You have a warning triangle. It should be displayed

Mark one answer
- [ ] A. on the roof of your vehicle
- [ ] B. at least 150 metres (492 feet) behind your vehicle
- [x] C. at least 45 metres (147 feet) behind your vehicle
- [ ] D. just behind your vehicle

805 You have stalled in the middle of a level crossing and cannot restart the engine. The warning bell starts to ring. You should

Mark one answer

- [ ] **A.** get out and clear of the crossing
- [ ] **B.** run down the track to warn the signal operator
- [ ] **C.** carry on trying to restart the engine
- [ ] **D.** push the vehicle clear of the crossing

806 You are on the motorway. Luggage falls from your vehicle. What should you do?

Mark one answer

- [ ] **A.** Stop at the next emergency telephone and contact the police
- [ ] **B.** Stop on the motorway and put on hazard lights whilst you pick it up
- [ ] **C.** Walk back up the motorway to pick it up
- [ ] **D.** Pull up on the hard shoulder and wave traffic down

807 You are on a motorway. When can you use hazard warning lights?

Mark two answers

- [ ] **A.** When a vehicle is following too closely
- [ ] **B.** When you slow down quickly because of danger ahead
- [ ] **C.** When you are towing another vehicle
- [ ] **D.** When driving on the hard shoulder
- [ ] **E.** When you have broken down on the hard shoulder

808 You are involved in an accident with another vehicle. Someone is injured. Your vehicle is damaged. Which FOUR of the following should you find out?

Mark four answers

- [x] **A.** Whether the driver owns the other vehicle involved
- [x] **B.** The other driver's name, address and telephone number
- [x] **C.** The make and registration number of the other vehicle
- [ ] **D.** The occupation of the other driver
- [x] **E.** The details of the other driver's vehicle insurance
- [ ] **F.** Whether the other driver is licensed to drive

809 You have broken down on a motorway. When you use the emergency telephone you will be asked

Mark three answers

- [x] **A.** for the number on the telephone that you are using
- [ ] **B.** for your driving licence details
- [ ] **C.** for the name of your vehicle insurance company
- [x] **D.** for details of yourself and your vehicle
- [x] **E.** whether you belong to a motoring organisation

810 At the scene of an accident you should

Mark one answer

- [x] **A.** not put yourself at risk
- [ ] **B.** go to those casualties who are screaming
- [ ] **C.** pull everybody out of their vehicles
- [ ] **D.** leave vehicle engines switched on

811
You are the first to arrive at the scene of an accident. Which FOUR of these should you do?

Mark four answers

- [ ] **A.** Leave as soon as another motorist arrives
- [x] **B.** Switch off the vehicle engine(s)
- [x] **C.** Move uninjured people away from the vehicle(s)
- [x] **D.** Call the emergency services
- [x] **E.** Warn other traffic

812
An accident has just happened. An injured person is lying in the busy road. What is the FIRST thing you should do to help?

Mark one answer

- [ ] **A.** Treat the person for shock
- [x] **B.** Warn other traffic
- [ ] **C.** Place them in the recovery position
- [ ] **D.** Make sure the injured person is kept warm

813
You are the first person to arrive at an accident where people are badly injured. Which THREE should you do?

Mark three answers

- [x] **A.** Switch on your own hazard warning lights
- [x] **B.** Make sure that someone telephones for an ambulance
- [ ] **C.** Try and get people who are injured to drink something
- [ ] **D.** Move the people who are injured clear of their vehicles
- [x] **E.** Get people who are not injured clear of the scene

814
You arrive at the scene of a motorcycle accident. The rider is injured. When should the helmet be removed?

Mark one answer

- [x] **A.** Only when it is essential
- [ ] **B.** Always straight away
- [ ] **C.** Only when the motorcyclist asks
- [ ] **D.** Always, unless they are in shock

815
You arrive at a serious motorcycle accident. The motorcyclist is unconscious and bleeding. Your main priorities should be to

Mark three answers

- [x] **A.** try to stop the bleeding
- [ ] **B.** make a list of witnesses
- [x] **C.** check the casualty's breathing
- [ ] **D.** take the numbers of the vehicles involved
- [ ] **E.** sweep up any loose debris
- [x] **F.** check the casualty's airways

816
You arrive at an accident. A motorcyclist is unconscious. Your FIRST priority is the casualty's

Mark one answer

- [x] **A.** breathing
- [ ] **B.** bleeding
- [ ] **C.** broken bones
- [ ] **D.** bruising

817 At an accident a casualty is unconscious. Which THREE of the following should you check urgently?

Mark three answers

- A. Circulation
- B. Airway
- C. Shock
- D. Breathing
- E. Broken bones

818 You arrive at the scene of an accident. It has just happened and someone is unconscious. Which of the following should be given urgent priority to help them?

Mark three answers

- A. Clear the airway and keep it open
- B. Try to get them to drink water
- C. Check that they are breathing
- D. Look for any witnesses
- E. Stop any heavy bleeding
- F. Take the numbers of vehicles involved

819 At an accident someone is unconscious. Your main priorities should be to

Mark three answers

- A. sweep up the broken glass
- B. take the names of witnesses
- C. count the number of vehicles involved
- D. check the airway is clear
- E. make sure they are breathing
- F. stop any heavy bleeding

820 You have stopped at the scene of an accident to give help. Which THREE things should you do?

Mark three answers

- ☑ A. Keep injured people warm and comfortable
- ☑ B. Keep injured people calm by talking to them reassuringly
- ☐ C. Keep injured people on the move by walking them around
- ☐ D. Give injured people a warm drink
- ☑ E. Make sure that injured people are not left alone

821 You arrive at the scene of an accident. It has just happened and someone is injured. Which THREE of the following should be given urgent priority?

Mark three answers

- ☑ A. Stop any severe bleeding
- ☐ B. Get them a warm drink
- ☑ C. Check that their breathing is OK
- ☐ D. Take numbers of vehicles involved
- ☐ E. Look for witnesses
- ☑ F. Clear their airway and keep it open

822 At an accident a casualty has stopped breathing. You should

Mark two answers

- ☑ A. remove anything that is blocking the mouth
- ☐ B. keep the head tilted forwards as far as possible
- ☐ C. raise the legs to help with circulation
- ☐ D. try to give the casualty something to drink
- ☑ E. keep the head tilted back as far as possible

823 You are at the scene of an accident. Someone is suffering from shock. You should

Mark four answers

- [x] A. reassure them constantly
- [ ] B. offer them a cigarette
- [x] C. keep them warm
- [x] D. avoid moving them if possible
- [x] E. loosen any tight clothing
- [ ] F. give them a warm drink

---

824 Which of the following should you NOT do at the scene of an accident?

Mark one answer

- [ ] A. Warn other traffic by switching on your hazard warning lights
- [ ] B. Call the emergency services immediately
- [x] C. Offer someone a cigarette to calm them down
- [ ] D. Ask drivers to switch off their engines

---

825 There has been an accident. The driver is suffering from shock. You should

Mark two answers

- [ ] A. give them a drink
- [x] B. reassure them
- [x] C. not leave them alone
- [ ] D. offer them a cigarette
- [ ] E. ask who caused the accident

---

826 You are at the scene of an accident. Someone is suffering from shock. You should

Mark three answers

- [ ] A. offer them a cigarette
- [ ] B. offer them a warm drink
- [x] C. keep them warm
- [x] D. loosen any tight clothing
- [x] E. reassure them constantly

---

827 You have to treat someone for shock at the scene of an accident. You should

Mark one answer

- [x] A. reassure them constantly
- [ ] B. walk them around to calm them down
- [ ] C. give them something cold to drink
- [ ] D. cool them down as soon as possible

---

828 You arrive at the scene of a motorcycle accident. No other vehicle is involved. The rider is unconscious, lying in the middle of the road. The first thing you should do is

Mark one answer

- [ ] A. move the rider out of the road
- [x] B. warn other traffic
- [ ] C. clear the road of debris
- [ ] D. give the rider reassurance

---

829 At an accident a small child is not breathing. When giving mouth to mouth you should breathe

Mark one answer

- [ ] A. sharply
- [x] B. gently
- [ ] C. heavily
- [ ] D. rapidly

---

830 To start mouth to mouth on a casualty you should

Mark three answers
- A. tilt their head forward
- B. clear the airway
- C. turn them on their side
- D. tilt their head back
- E. pinch the nostrils together
- F. put their arms across their chest

831 When you are giving mouth to mouth you should only stop when

Mark one answer
- A. you think the casualty is dead
- B. the casualty can breathe without help
- C. the casualty has turned blue
- D. you think the ambulance is coming

832 You arrive at the scene of an accident. There has been an engine fire and someone's hands and arms have been burnt. You should NOT

Mark one answer
- A. douse the burn thoroughly with cool liquid
- B. lay the casualty down
- C. remove anything sticking to the burn
- D. reassure them constantly

833 You arrive at an accident where someone is suffering from severe burns. You should

Mark one answer
- A. apply lotions to the injury
- B. burst any blisters
- C. remove anything stuck to the burns
- D. douse the burns with cool liquid

834 You arrive at an accident where someone is suffering from severe burns. You should

Mark one answer
- A. burst any blisters
- B. douse the burns thoroughly with cool liquid ✓
- C. apply lotions to the injury
- D. remove anything sticking to the burns

835 You arrive at the scene of an accident. A pedestrian has a severe bleeding wound on their leg, although it is not broken. What should you do?

Mark two answers
- A. Dab the wound to stop bleeding
- B. Keep both legs flat on the ground
- C. Apply firm pressure to the wound ✓
- D. Raise the leg to lessen bleeding ✓
- E. Fetch them a warm drink

836 You arrive at the scene of an accident. A passenger is bleeding badly from an arm wound. What should you do?

Mark one answer
- A. Apply pressure over the wound and keep the arm down
- B. Dab the wound
- C. Get them a drink
- D. Apply pressure over the wound and raise the arm ✓

837 You arrive at the scene of an accident. A pedestrian is bleeding heavily from a leg wound but the leg is not broken. What should you do?

Mark one answer
- A. Dab the wound to stop the bleeding
- B. Keep both legs flat on the ground
- C. Apply firm pressure to the wound
- D. Fetch them a warm drink

838 At an accident a casualty is unconscious but still breathing. You should only move them if

Mark one answer
- A. an ambulance is on its way
- B. bystanders advise you to
- C. there is further danger
- D. bystanders will help you to

839 At an accident you suspect a casualty has back injuries. The area is safe. You should

Mark one answer
- A. offer them a drink
- B. not move them
- C. raise their legs
- D. offer them a cigarette

840 At an accident it is important to look after the casualty. When the area is safe, you should

Mark one answer
- A. get them out of the vehicle
- B. give them a drink
- C. give them something to eat
- D. keep them in the vehicle

841 A tanker is involved in an accident. Which sign would show that the tanker is carrying dangerous goods?

Mark one answer
- A. LONG VEHICLE
- B. 2YE 1089
- C.
- D.

842 For which THREE should you use your hazard warning lights?

Mark three answers
- A. When you are parking in a restricted area
- B. When you are temporarily obstructing traffic
- C. To warn following traffic of a hazard ahead
- D. When you have broken down
- E. When only stopping for a short time

843 The police may ask you to produce which three of these documents following an accident?

Mark three answers

- A. Vehicle registration document
- B. Driving licence
- C. Theory test certificate
- D. Insurance certificate
- E. MOT test certificate
- F. Road tax disc

844 At a railway level crossing the red light signal continues to flash after a train has gone by. What should you do?

Mark one answer

- A. Phone the signal operator
- B. Alert drivers behind you
- C. Wait
- D. Proceed with caution

845 You see a car on the hard shoulder of a motorway with a HELP pennant displayed. This means the driver is most likely to be

Mark one answer

- A. a disabled person
- B. first aid trained
- C. a foreign visitor
- D. a rescue patrol person

846 On the motorway the hard shoulder should be used

Mark one answer

- A. to answer a mobile phone
- B. when an emergency arises
- C. for a short rest when tired
- D. to check a road atlas

847 For which TWO should you use hazard warning lights?

Mark two answers

- A. When you slow down quickly on a motorway because of a hazard ahead
- B. When you have broken down
- C. When you wish to stop on double yellow lines
- D. When you need to park on the pavement

848 When are you allowed to use hazard warning lights?

Mark one answer

- A. When stopped and temporarily obstructing traffic
- B. When travelling during darkness without headlights
- C. When parked for shopping on double yellow lines
- D. When travelling slowly because you are lost

849 You are on a motorway. A large box falls onto the road from a lorry. The lorry does not stop. You should

Mark one answer

- A. go to the next emergency telephone and inform the police
- B. catch up with the lorry and try to get the driver's attention
- C. stop close to the box until the police arrive
- D. pull over to the hard shoulder, then remove the box

850 Any load that is carried on a roof rack MUST be

Mark one answer

- [x] **A.** securely fastened when driving
- [ ] **B.** carried only when strictly necessary
- [ ] **C.** as light as possible
- [ ] **D.** covered with plastic sheeting

851 Which THREE are suitable restraints for a child under three years?

Mark three answers

- [x] **A.** A child seat
- [ ] **B.** An adult holding a child
- [ ] **C.** An adult seat belt
- [ ] **D.** A lap belt
- [x] **E.** A harness
- [x] **F.** A baby carrier

852 Your vehicle is fitted with child safety door locks. You should use these so that children inside the car cannot open

Mark one answer

- [ ] **A.** the right-hand doors
- [ ] **B.** the left-hand doors
- [x] **C.** the rear doors
- [ ] **D.** any of the doors

853 You are planning to tow a caravan. Which of these will mostly help to aid the vehicle handling?

Mark one answer

- [ ] **A.** A jockey-wheel fitted to the towbar
- [ ] **B.** Power steering fitted to the towing vehicle
- [ ] **C.** Anti-lock brakes fitted to the towing vehicle
- [x] **D.** A stabiliser fitted to the towbar

854 If a trailer swerves or snakes when you are towing it you should

Mark one answer

- [x] **A.** ease off the accelerator and reduce your speed
- [ ] **B.** let go of the steering wheel and let it correct itself
- [ ] **C.** brake hard and hold the pedal down
- [ ] **D.** increase your speed as quickly as possible

855 How can you stop a caravan snaking from side to side?

Mark one answer

- [ ] **A.** Turn the steering wheel slowly to each side
- [ ] **B.** Accelerate to increase your speed
- [ ] **C.** Stop as quickly as you can
- [x] **D.** Slow down very gradually

856 On which TWO occasions might you inflate your tyres to more than the recommended normal pressure?

Mark two answers

- A. When the roads are slippery
- ☑ B. When driving fast for a long distance
- C. When the tyre tread is worn below 2mm
- ☑ D. When carrying a heavy load
- E. When the weather is cold
- F. When the vehicle is fitted with anti-lock brakes

857 A heavy load on your roof rack will

Mark one answer

- A. improve the road holding
- B. reduce the stopping distance
- C. make the steering lighter
- ☑ D. reduce stability

858 Are passengers allowed to ride in a caravan that is being towed?

Mark one answer

- A. Yes if they are over fourteen
- ☑ B. No not at any time
- C. Only if all the seats in the towing vehicle are full
- D. Only if a stabiliser is fitted

859 You are towing a caravan along a motorway. The caravan begins to swerve from side to side. What should you do?

Mark one answer

- ☑ A. Ease off the accelerator slowly
- B. Steer sharply from side to side
- C. Do an emergency stop
- D. Speed up very quickly

860 A trailer must stay securely hitched-up to the towing vehicle. What additional safety device can be fitted to the trailer braking system?

Mark one answer

- A. Stabiliser
- B. Jockey wheel
- C. Corner steadies
- ☑ D. Breakaway cable

861 Overloading your vehicle can seriously affect the

Mark two answers

- A. gearbox
- ☑ B. steering
- ☑ C. handling
- D. battery life
- E. journey time

862 Who is responsible for making sure that a vehicle is not overloaded?

Mark one answer

- A. The driver of the vehicle
- B. The owner of the items being carried
- C. The person who loaded the vehicle
- D. The licensing authority

863 You are towing a small trailer on a busy three-lane motorway. All the lanes are open. You must

Mark two answers

- A. not exceed 60mph
- B. not overtake
- C. have a stabiliser fitted
- D. use only the left and centre lanes